STUDYING FILMS

STUDYING TALK TO HER

Emily Hughes

First published in 2015 by
Auteur, 24 Hartwell Crescent, Leighton Buzzard LU7 1NP
www.auteur.co.uk

Copyright © Auteur Publishing 2015

Designed and set by Nikki Hamlett at Cassels Design www.casselsdesign.co.uk

British Library Cataloguing-in-Publication Data
A catalogue record for this book is available from the British Library

ISBN: 978-0-9932384-0-6 paperback
ISBN: 978-0-9932384-1-3 ebook

Printed and bound by CPI Group (UK) Ltd, Croydon, CR0 4YY

Contents

Fact Sheet for *Talk to Her*

Director & Screenplay: Pedro Almodóvar

Executive Producer: Augustín Almodóvar

Associate Producer: Michel Ruben

Music: Alberto Iglesias

Cinematography: Javier Aguirresarobe

Editing: José Salcedo

Release date: Spain 15th March 2002

UK 23rd August 2002

USA 25th December 2002

Lead actors: Benigno (Javier Cámara), Marco (Darío Grandinetti), Alicia (Leonor Watling), and Lydia (Rosario Flores)

Plot Synopsis of *Talk to Her* (Plot Spoiler Alert!)

The film starts in the theatre at a dance performance. Benigno notices a man (Marco) sitting next to him, crying. The scene cuts to a hospital where Benigno, a nurse, washes a woman in a coma (Alicia). Benigno tells the comatose Alicia about the dance performance. Marco watches TV and sees Lydia, a female bullfighter, having an argument with the host of a chat show. Marco decides to do a feature on Lydia. He goes to Lydia's next bullfight and watches from the crowd as Lydia triumphs. Marco meets her and gives her a lift home. He drops her home and kills a snake in her kitchen. A title comes up on the screen: 'Several months later.' Marco and Lydia (now a couple) drive to a bullfight. Lydia gets dressed into her Matador's costume and enters the arena; she is quickly gored by the bull. Lydia, now in a coma, is taken to El Bosque hospital; Marco sits at her bedside. The scene cuts to a flashback of Lydia and Marco at a party listening to Spanish guitar music. Marco cries and tells Lydia about Angela (his ex) and her phobia of snakes. Back in the present, Marco lingers at the door of Alicia's hospital door and Benigno invites him in. Benigno reveals that he remembers Marco from the theatre; they become friends. Benigno tells Marco about how he came to care for Alicia. The flashback begins with Benigno at the window looking out over the dance studio. One day, Alicia drops her wallet and Benigno runs down to give it back and walks her home. He arranges an appointment with her father who is a psychologist and tells him about his unusual upbringing caring for his mother. After the appointment, Benigno sneaks into Alicia's room and steals a hair clip. Benigno later learns Alicia has been in a car accident and is in a coma. Dr Roncero employs Benigno to care for Alicia day and night. One night, Benigno tells the comatose Alicia about a film he saw. 'The Shrinking Lover' about Amparo, a scientist, who is making a diet formula. Her boyfriend Alfredo drinks the formula to prove he is not selfish and begins to shrink. Alfredo goes away and years later, now around eight inches tall, Amparo finds him to rescue him. On their first night back together, as Amparo sleeps, Alfredo crawls on top of her naked body, finds her vagina and enters to live there forever. The scene then cuts to a month later, Alicia and Lydia are on the balcony with Benigno and Marco, Benigno imagines the two are talking about them. The scene cuts to a flash back of Angela's wedding. Marco insists it is over between him and Angela and tells Lydia about their relationship. Back in the present, Marco returns to Lydia's room to find El Niño who tells Marco about Lydia's affair with him. Rosa notices that Alicia has not had her period. Marco is outraged when Benigno reveals to him that he wants to marry Alicia. They are overheard by a colleague. It is later revealed that Alicia has been raped and is pregnant. Benigno is the prime suspect. Eight months later Marco reads that Lydia has died. Marco calls the clinic and Rosa informs him that Benigno is in jail accused of raping Alicia. Marco visits Benigno in jail and Benigno offers him his flat. Marco looks out the window at the dance studio and sees that Alicia is now awake. Marco visits Benigno's lawyer who tells him that the baby was born dead and that Benigno should not be told that Alicia has woken up. Benigno takes an overdose of sleeping pills intending to put him in a coma; he dies. Marco visits his grave and tells him Alicia is alive. The film ends as it begins, in the theatre. During the interval Marco sees Alicia who smiles and asks him if he is OK. A title comes on the screen: 'Marco y Alicia'. The film ends with a third and final dance sequence.

Introduction

Talk to Her (*Hable con Ella*) (2002) is a vastly rich and interesting film, which begs to be analysed in depth. The film won the 2003 Oscar for best original screenplay and has been hailed as Almodóvar's masterpiece.[1] The film offers much both in terms of thematic analysis and micro analysis of the sound, performance, **cinematography**, **editing** and *mise-en-scène*. Like most of Almodóvar's films, little is clear cut; the characters are complex and our affinity and empathy for them shifts throughout the film.

Almodóvar is Spain's most famous, prolific and celebrated contemporary director and any study of his films cannot be complete without considering the social context of Spain. In a style which has been referred to as postmodernist, *Talk to Her*'s Spain is a mongrel; a mix of the traditional and modern. Spanish guitars and bull fighting mingle with a hyper-real mishmash of 60s wallpaper, expressive dance and crass TV chat shows.

Almodóvar can be considered to be a director who is a specialist in gender and the issue of gender identity is explored in *Talk to Her*, particularly the notion that gender characteristics are fluid and not fixed. Almodóvar's characters simultaneously embody and reject gender stereotypes and share both feminine and masculine attributes.

The film contains **themes** present within many of Almodóvar's films such as loneliness, communication, the impossibility of a romantic relationship and psychology. Physicality and the body are central to Almodóvar's films and particularly to *Talk to Her*; a film which explores both the active and passive body. Further to this, the issue of spectatorship is important in relation to how the body is presented to and interpreted by the spectator and how this gaze at times celebrates, sexualises, objectifies and medicalises the human form; especially the nude.

Almodóvar self-consciously both celebrates and rejects traditional **genre** and **narrative** conventions and as such, the film offers a rich opportunities for analysis in these frameworks. The film can be considered simultaneously both 'genreless' and rich with conventions from many genres. Almodóvar's attitude to narrative structure is playful, winding backwards and forwards in time through the two relationships.

Most of all, what makes *Talk to Her* such an interesting film to dissect, is the uneasy position that Almodóvar places the spectator in and how its messages and values create moral ambiguity. The film delivers morally complex, hazy messages about rape, **voyeurism** and obsession and consequently, the spectator finds humour where they should find revulsion and sympathy where they should find anger. Our attitudes towards characters and events can change dramatically from first screening to close analysis. As a result, the film has sparked a great deal of critical, theoretical and philosophical analysis particularly around the issue of rape.

The film was generally well received by critics and audiences and there is an extensive amount of analysis of the film from a range of different perspectives from bloggers to philosophers, psychologists to dance/ performance theorists. The aim of this book is to bring together many of the interpretations and discourses surrounding the film in a readable and easy to digest way.

Just as the last lines of the film are 'Nothing is simple' so, too, the whole film can be thought of as complicated. However it is within the complexity of the film that one can find the most interest in the film. So much of the visual symbolism and the **dialogue** from the Oscar winning screenplay within the film is polysemic, and in this book I aim to suggest different interpretations rather than focusing on one argument or point of view.

One of the great things about studying Almodóvar's films is that they are wide open to interpretation and, as the reader of this book, I hope that you will be able to form your own opinions on the messages, genre, narrative, characters and themes of *Talk to Her* as well as engaging with notions of auteurship, spectatorship and the Spanish historical and social context. As Almodóvar said:

> One of the wonderful things about film is that it can be seen in a thousand different ways, all of them real. You have to be flexible with a movie and with life in general [...] you have to be tolerant and you have to have a sense of humour, and you don't have to accept things on face value.[2]

References

1. www.rollingstone.com/movies/reviews/talk-to-her-20021105 (accessed 10/09/14)

2. http://www.filmmakermagazine.com/ archives/issues/spring1994/pedro.php#. VBCxAPIdXwg (accessed 08/09/14)

Almodóvar as an Auteur

Paul Julian Smith refers to Almodóvar as 'the one true auteur to emerge from the 80's'[1] and Martin D'Lugo refers to him as 'an undisputable international auteur'.[2] **Auteur** was a word first used in France in the 1960's where writers of the film magazine *Cahiers du Cinema* coined the term to describe a growing number of directors whom they considered to have a signature style across several of their films. This signature could be in the form of a visual style through reoccurring **motifs** and techniques within the cinematography, *mise-en-scène* or editing or through sound, themes, **representations**, genre, narrative or the inclusion of similar characters. There seems to be overwhelming evidence to suggest that, across the nineteen feature films made up until 2013, Almodóvar has defining and **reoccurring tropes** in *all* of these categories.

Throughout the book, there will be constant reference to the qualities and characteristics of *Talk to Her* that adhere to Almodóvar's auteur style, however it is important to understand where some of the qualities and characteristics of his work emerge from.

Almodóvar in Historical and Social Context

Almodóvar made his first appearance as a filmmaker in the late seventies during a period of immense cultural and political upheaval. However, the story of the Spanish film industry as a whole is equally turbulent.

While the early days of the moving image from the late nineteenth century up until 1935 were much the same in Spain as they were in the rest of Western Europe, the change from an agricultural society to an industrial one in Spain was slower. As a consequence, much of the early Spanish cinema industry centred around the cities of Madrid and Barcelona with film-makers such as Luis Buñuel (director of *Viridiana* (1961) - see the section on Rape in Spanish Cinema) finding artistic success. Many of the films of this early era were, as Jordan and Allinson note, involved in 'recycling 'Deep Spain' i.e. films heavy in Spanish **iconography**, this early tradition may have been an influence on Almodóvar's own 'recycling' of Spanish iconography in *Talk to Her*.[3]

As Sally Faulkner notes, the introduction of sound was 'disastrous for this developing Spanish Cinema'[4] with many film-makers moving to Hollywood to take part in this new emerging technology. Sound also posed a problem for European cinema more generally. With so many different languages in Europe, films were hard to export and share between different countries. In 1931 only one Spanish film was made as audiences turned to the technological spectacle of imported Hollywood sound cinema. Equally, the film industry was affected by the impact of the Great Depression upon the Spanish economy. In the mid 1930's the industry had picked up again with film production companies like Filmófono and CIFESA beginning to make more Spanish films for Spanish audiences. This peak was short lived. The outbreak of civil war in 1936 saw a huge change in the film industry with film now being a powerful tool for **political propaganda**.

The Spanish Civil War, 1936-39, was fought between the Nationalists who supported General Francisco Franco (allied with the fascist regimes of Mussolini in Italy and Hitler in Germany) who believed in traditional values of religion, monarchy and preserving Spanish national identity, versus the Republicans (supported by France and Great Britain) who supported the democratically elected Spanish Republic Party. The war was brutal, taking an approximate 500,000 victims[5] and shaking the foundations of Spanish society. Franco and his fascist Nationalist party won and brought in a Nationalist regime which lasted for nearly forty years until his Franco's death in 1975. Under the regime, people who criticised society and politics were often imprisoned. Religions other than Catholicism were not tolerated and elements that were considered 'un-Spanish' were repressed. As a consequence, sports like bullfighting and dances like the Flamenco were heavily promoted. Regional languages and dialects were no longer officially recognised in an attempt to try and build a single Spanish national identity. Whereas by the 50's and 60's, women in the rest of Western Europe were gaining greater independence, particularly within the realm of education and employment, Franco's regime encouraged traditional family units where women took on more domestic roles. Homosexuality was illegal and legalised after Franco's death in 1979. Films and all other cultural output in Spain had to pass strict censorship rules and any content that seemed to criticise the regime or have anti Catholic, **communist**, **liberal** or **gender progressive** messages were subject to censorship. Jordan and Allinson describe some of the censorship problems facing film-makers during the Franco Era:

Film censorship was rolled out nation-wide after July 1939. Within its remit were tasks such as the pre-censorship of all submitted film scripts, the approval of shooting scripts and exhibition licences for Spanish films, the imposition of cuts and changes to sound and image tracks in completed films, the authorisation of subtitling or dubbing plus film classification.[6]

Despite this, the Franco regime did recognise the potential of film in reflecting Spanish national identity and during the 1960s government sponsored film schools were set up such as The Official Film School. As Faulkner notes, the Franco regime was keen for film to be a medium of quality and as such, many Spanish films were made with the intention that they be entered into foreign **film festivals** such as Cannes.[7] The whole system was filled with bureaucracy and as a consequence, born in 1949, the films that Almodóvar would have watched in his youth would either have been those that gave a biased, uncritical, traditional vision of Spain or, they would have been foreign, mainly American films that did not challenge the **ideology** of the Franco regime.

La Movida Madrileña

Franco's death in 1975 not only caused immense political upheaval, in the formation of a new democratic system of government, but also lead to a cultural movement La Movida Madrileña. Almodóvar was at the heart of the movement which was typified by: experimentation in gender identity, youth culture, colour, cultural innovation and the popularity of 60's and 70's pop art and punk styles in fashion and interior decor. Paula Willoquet-Maricondi described La Movida as 'a rising 'new Spanish mentality' bent on overcoming boundaries and taboos'.[8] The period was a reaction against all that had repressed under Franco. It was an era of **hedonism**, creative expression, tolerance of new kinds of **subcultures** and sexual orientations. Almodóvar describes this era:

> It's difficult to speak of La Movida and explain it to those who didn't live those years. We weren't a generation; we weren't an artistic movement; we weren't a group with a concrete ideology. We were simply a bunch of people that coincided in one of the most explosive moments in the country.[9]

Almodóvar was a central part of the La Movida Madrileña movement both in its instigation and in chronicling its development. He wrote comic books and sung in a glam rock **parody** band alongside Fabio McNamara. He directed and acted in his own short films made on Super 8 cameras which were shown at parties and bars in Barcelona and, the city at the heart of La Movida, Madrid. He wrote articles about the movement for the newspaper El Pais and countercultural magazines such as Vibraciones thus arguably giving the movement more social and cultural recognition and significance. He directed his first feature length film five years after Franco's death. *Pepi, Luci, Bom and other Girls on the Heap* (1980) is a riotous collage of hedonism, sexual exploration and the punk aesthetic which reflects the party culture and sexual openness of the new Madrid. Similarly, his 1987 film *Law of Desire* explores the impact of La Movida by exploring the growing openness to different sexual experiences (notably orgies) and the growing tolerance towards homosexuality by featuring gay relationships.

La Movida and the general shift in politics and culture had a huge impact on the gender roles in Spanish society. Almodóvar grew up in a very female centred and lead community which was in contrast to the **patriarchal** nature of Franco lead society across Spain. Although his father was a constant figure in his life, it is, for the majority of his films, his mother and his sisters whom he seems to be more inspired by. As Suzie Mackenzie states Almodóvar's 'entire career has been devoted to subverting images of power'.[10] The image of power for much of Almodóvar's childhood would have been male in the form of the Franco regime, the Civil Guard (Franco's military police force) and the Catholic Church. Like many of Almodóvar's other films such as *High Heels* (1991), *All About My Mother* (1999), *Bad Education* (2004) and *The Skin I Live In* (2011), *Talk to Her* deals with the refusal to accept traditional gender roles which can be considered a central and defining feature of Almodóvar's auteur status.

Whilst the hedonism and excess of some of his earlier films are somewhat repressed in *Talk to Her*, there are hints of La Movida's influence in some of the secondary characters such as the flamboyant talk show host and through the *mise-en-scène* and **colour palette** of the film. The theme of rebirth and rebirth being caused by a death is central to *Talk to Her* and somewhat mirrors the cultural rebirth of Spain after the death of Franco. In a general sense La Movida may have influenced Almodóvar to continually push boundaries, explore taboo subjects and play with gender and traditional images of power.

The Early 2000s

Whilst Almodóvar's films are firmly rooted in Spanish culture and are influenced by Spain's history, to a certain extent the immediate social context of the early 2000's when it was made, could be seen as fairly irrelevant as *Talk to Her* can be considered quite classical and timeless in its messages and themes. Additionally, in the vein of many of his films, it could be considered fairly **apolitical** in that is does not engage with the social issues of everyday Spaniards.

Sally Faulkner asserts that during the late 1990s Almodóvar reinvented himself from a director working on shoe string budgets and with risky, sometimes grotesque subject matter, to a director who, as Faulkner asserts made themselves much more appealing to the 'middlebrow';[11] a middleclass and culturally literate audience. She states that this change occurred first with the film *The Flower of My Secret* (1995) which took him from being an outsider to having 'an immeasurable contribution [...] to the cultural prestige of Modern Spain'.[12]

Faulkner argues that this change owes as much to the institutional context in which Almodóvar's films were made as it does to Almodóvar's maturity as a director. During the 1990's a system of **government subsidy** was set up in order to encourage greater quality within the Spanish film industry. Faulkner describes, that the impact of this was to encourage a certain style of film making:

> While the aim was change, whereby directors were freed from the constraints of censorship and lack of financing [...] the Film Protection Fund could easily be seen as a new form of censorship: certain films were favoured, others were discouraged.[13]

She states that the kind of films that were encouraged were: 'left wing, with auteurist directors and the potential to win prizes at foreign film festivals' and 'quality cinema with high budgets'.[14] Although *Talk to Her* is not government funded (unlike some of Almodóvar's other films) *Talk to Her* certainly fits many of the descriptions of the *type* of cinema that the Spanish government in the late 1990s early 2000s were trying to cultivate. The film has an auteurist feel to it and was nominated for and won several awards including a BAFTA, a Golden Globe and an Academy Award. It could be seen to fit into the idea of 'quality cinema' through its complexity but also through the fact that the film's micro elements of sound, cinematography, *mise-en-scène* and editing can be thought of as technically proficient and visually pleasing. Writing for Sight and Sound Magazine, Paul Julian Smith says that Talk to Her 'signals the start of a new, ambitious and risky period for Almodóvar'[15] commenting upon the change to a more subtle, complex and artistic phase in his career. This phase would continue into his subsequent critically acclaimed films *Bad Education*, *Volver* (2006), *Broken Embraces* (2009) *The Skin I Live In* and end somewhat with *I'm So Excited!* (2013) which is potentially less subtle, more flamboyant and brash perhaps in the style of his earlier films.

Almodóvar's 'Club'

Almodóvar both writes and directs his films and keeps things in the family with many of his films being produced by his brother Augustín. Almodóvar likes to use many of the same crew and the same actors in his films and indeed, in one scene where Marco and Lydia are listening to Spanish guitar music (a scene that does little to develop the plot), the camera **pans** through the audience revealing actresses from his previous films Marisa Paredes *The Flower of My Secret*, *The Skin I Live In* and *Dark Habits* (1983) and Cecilia Roth of *Labyrinth of Passion* (1982) , *All About My Mother*, *Dark Habits* and who would go on to be in *I'm So Excited!* The film also has a cameo from Chus Lampreave another of Almodóvar's favoured actresses, who plays Benigno's building manager. One gets the sense from scenes like these that Almodóvar is not only the darling of the Spanish film industry but, his auteur status is like a club with similar actors, crew and settings featuring across several of his films.

El Deseo

Unlike most Hollywood directors whose status as an auteur can often be brought into question by the mediation of cast and crew and the pressures of the producer and the studio, Almodóvar owns his own movie studio. Founded in 1985/6 El Deseo (meaning Desire), was set up initially to produce *Law of Desire* (1987) and has produced all of Almodóvar's subsequent films. Not only does this allow Almodóvar and his brother Augustín to direct and produce their own films but, they are also able to enhance Spanish cinema as a whole, as they help support, produce and fund films made by other Spanish and Latin American directors such as Guillermo Del Torro's *The Devil's Backbone* (2001) which was produced by Augustín Almodóvar and executive produced by Pedro Almodóvar.

Upon visiting El Deseo, journalist Adam Woodward writing for Little White Lies magazine writes about the creative environment at the studio describing it as:

> ...a sensual banquet [...] a kaleidoscopic metropolis of colour and light. [...]The place has an infectious, harmonious energy about it.[16]

El Deseo is significant in considering Almodóvar as an auteur. Like other auteur directors who own their own companies such as Quentin Tarantino (A Band Apart), Baz Luhrman (Bazmark Inc.) and Ridley Scott (Scott Free), Almodóvar is able to cultivate a creative space in his own vision which fits his own requirements as a film-maker.

As Paul Julian Smith notes from a private conversation with Augustín Almodóvar, owning their own film production company allows for their films to be **shot in sequence**, i.e. in roughly the chronological order that they will appear in the film; 'thus following the natural development of character and narrative'[17]. This way of filming rarely occurs in Hollywood cinema whose productions are restricted by tight financial budgets, crew and cast's diaries, locations and strict time frames. In *Talk to Her*, characters like Benigno and Alicia not only transform as characters, but also physically transform so filming in this way arguably adds a depth and richness to the performances.

Challenges to seeing Almodóvar as an Auteur

As much as *Talk to Her* has many of the hallmarks of an 'Almodóvar film', the film poses some interesting challenges in being seen as an auteur film. To a certain extent, Almodóvar breaks patterns within *Talk to*

Her. Almodóvar is often described as a women's director or, an **LGBTQ** director. *Talk to Her* disrupts this trend by having two heterosexual males as the main **protagonists**. The film as a whole could be described as a tale of male friendship with women talking on a lesser role and homosexuals non-existent within the plot.

Secondly, arguably the style that Almodóvar makes his films in, filming in chronological order, means that much of the craft in structuring the narrative lies with his editor José Salcedo who also worked on *Volver* and *All About My Mother*. Thus El Deseo and its regular crew might better be given auteur status that just Almodóvar alone. Indeed, in his interview in Little White Lies he acknowledges the impact that others have had on his films stating:

> I don't have that certainty when I start a film because a film is a living being itself, it has a life of itself, and it's full of other people as well. Those people can also influence the direction that the film moves in and you have to be constantly keeping tabs and making sure you're in control of the film in case it's been led elsewhere.[18]

Equally, as most of Almodóvar's films have been produced by his brother Augustín, we could consider the auteur status to be attributed to a partnership in the style of other sibling auteurs such as the American directors Joel and Ethan Cohen.

Although *Talk to Her* has some aspects which are unmistakably 'Almodóvarian' such as gaudy interior decor, melodramatic acting, and brash, colourful characters. *Talk to Her* as a whole is arguably less floridly flamboyant and brash than some of his earlier films. The film is arguably more sensitive, with more depth to its characters.

References

1. Julian Smith, Paul. (2014) *Desire Unlimited: The Cinema of Pedro Almodóvar*. London: Verso. p. 5

2. D'Lugo, Marvin. (2006) *Contemporary Film-makers: Pedro Almodóvar*. USA: University of Illinois Press

3. Jordan, Barry and Allinson, Mark (2005) *Spanish Cinema a Student's Guide*. London: Hodder Arnold. p. 6

4. Faulkner, Sally. (2013) *A History of Spanish Film: Cinema and Society 1910-2010*. London: Bloomsbury Academic. p. 17

5. Lannon, Francis. (2003) *The Spanish Civil War, 1936-1939*. Oxford: Osprey Publishing. p. 7

6. Jordan, Barry and Allinson, Mark. p. 15

7. Faulkner, p. 17

8. Paula Willoquet-Maricondi. (2004) *Pedro Almodóvar: Interviews*. USA University Press of Mississippi. p. xi

9. Almodóvar, quoted in the introduction to PEPI, LUCI, BOM on the Optimum DVD: Almodóvar Collection, Vol. 1

10. Mackenzie, Suzie in Edt. Paula Willoquet-Maricondi. (2004) *Pedro Almodóvar: Interviews*. USA University Press of Mississippi. p. 155

11. Faulkner, p. 217

12. Faulkner, p. 162

13. Faulkner, p. 161

14. Faulkner, p. 161

15. Julian Smith, p. 174

16. Woodward, Adam. (23rd August 2011) *Pedro Almodóvar www.littlewhitelies.co.uk/features/articles/pedro-almodovar-16259* (accessed 19/09/14)

17. Julian Smith, p. 4

18. Woodward, ibid.

Mise-en-scène and Cinematography

Intertextuality

Almodóvar had no formal training within film and as a consequence, he has learnt his craft by watching films as an avid cinephile. Almodóvar's **mise-en-scène** is rich with **intertextual** references, whether it be from high culture, with his inclusion of choreography from the renowned choreographer Piña Bausch at the start and end of *Talk to Her*, through the **pastiche** of other films such as *The Devil Doll* (1936) and *The Incredible Shrinking Man* (1957), or through the *mise-en-scène* and the symbolism of props and costume. He states: *'For me, the films I see become part of my own experiences, and I use them as such.'*[1]

Heavily used visual motifs such as 'the Matador' occur frequently in *Talk to Her* perhaps in **homage** and parody of the traditional Spanish iconography encouraged under the Franco regime. Similarly, Almodóvar is renowned for drawing upon and being influenced by Hollywood directors of the 1950's such as Alfred Hitchcock and Douglas Sirk and one can see influences from both of these directors work in the film through the performances, bright colour palettes and themes. Like the **melodrama** films of the 50's and like the cinema of Hitchcock, Almodóvar's unique and distinctive style is classified by a somewhat obsessive attention to *mise-en-scène*. This is most noticeable in the domestic settings. Almodóvar pays close attention to objects, colour, painting and product design much of which has deeper symbolism and meaning, thus close analysis of stills from the film can be fruitful in revealing more about characters and themes

Mise-en-scène and Setting

Almodóvar commonly uses institutional settings such as hospitals (in *Law of Desire* and *All About My Mother*), airports and airplanes (in *High Heels* and *I'm So Excited!*) and prisons (in *High Heels* and *Talk to Her*) all, with hyper-realistic, colourful and **kitsch** production design. Almodóvar's *mise-en-scène* often has a warm and vibrant colour palette and a fun pop art inspired interior decor. In *Talk to Her* Almodóvar takes the hospital setting, a space normally associated with clinical greys, whites, murky greens and blues and makes it into a warm, vibrant, homely place.

Almodóvar's hospital is painted in a 'sienna mustard'[2] the same colour that Alicia's bedroom was painted, and the same colour that Benigno paints the flat he is preparing for him and Alicia. The implication is thus that potentially Alicia has an equally warm personality. This colour has been used in other Almodóvar domestic settings in *Broken Embraces* and *All About My Mother* always to create warmth and intimacy within a space.

Symptomatic *Mise-en-scène*

Almodóvar uses *mise-en-scène* to help him develop back-stories to add depth and gravity to his characters. He describes the *mise-en-scène* in Alicia's room:

> [Alicia had] an alarm clock and a photo of her parents when they were young. And two tiny brightly coloured boats, a souvenir which Katerina bought her from a trip she'd made to Salvador de Bahia to see the Bahian women dance.[3]

Almodóvar's use of *mise-en-scène*, most notably props, can be described as **symptomatic *mise-en-scène***; where the costumes, colour palette, setting and design give us non-verbal clues about the characters. Like the 1950's Hollywood melodrama films of Douglas Sirk, the *mise-en-scène* in *Talk to Her* is employed as a narrative device. John Mercer and Martin Shingler state that in melodrama symptomatic *mise-en-scène* helps to 'fill the absences created by what cannot be said or demonstrated by characters.'[4] Thus, symptomatic *mise-en-scène* is used within *Talk to Her* film to communicate and develop the female characters who have relatively few lines of dialogue.

We hear Benigno's mother but never see her. Through the *mise-en-scène* we learn more about her. In the background of one of the shots in Benigno's house there is a wedding photograph of Benigno's mother; however, the groom appears to have been cut off with only a fragment remaining (Fig. 1). Within the image there is an interesting story; an insight into Benigno's fragmented family life. The image tells us about the lack of father figure within Benigno's upbringing and gives us an insight into his mother's relationships with men. Perhaps this is what she reduces men to, a fragment or sliver of masculinity.

Fig. 1

In *Talk to Her*, Alicia quite literally cannot speak or demonstrate her personality throughout the majority of the film, and she has relatively little dialogue when she is awake, thus elements of the *mise-en-scène* are used to help create her backstory and develop her character. The *mise-en-scène* during the scene in Alicia's house (some of which is also in her hospital room) tells us about her character and is presented to us through **point-of-view** shots from Benigno's perspective as he sneaks into her room after visiting her father.

As Benigno walks into Alicia's room the *mise-en-scène* is rich with visual information (Fig. 2). Firstly to Benigno's right, the door is adorned with childish cut out letters similar to that of a toddler's room. Behind Benigno is a collection of small tin cars. Both props infantilise Alicia making her later rape even more shocking. To Benigno's left, partially in view, is a poster for Fritz Lang's *Metropolis* (1927). The film poster links to Alicia's, and then by inheritance, Benigno's, interest in silent cinema. The poster holds an added significance, Benigno is entering Alicia's private space (adorned with an image silent cinema) without consent; a symbolic rape. Later during the actual rape sequence, silent cinema is present again, this time as a masking device.

Fig. 2

On one of the bedside tables is the lava lamp, a pervasive motif within the film that takes on a sexual connotation during the rape scene. The lamp is a kitsch throwback to the 1960's and 70's *mise-en-scène* that Almodóvar likes to use in lots of his films. Next to it is a model of the Eiffel tower signifying her love of travel. On Alicia's wall we see black and white photographs of dancers (Fig. 3). The image may well be from one of Piña Bausch's productions and seems to echo the style of the signed image of Piña Bausch that Benigno gives her after the first Café Müller dance performance. The images clearly echo some of the other themes and images in the film about the interplay of men and women and further reinforce the importance of dance in Alicia's life.

In a point-of-view shot the camera tracks across one of shelves in the room and stops upon a number of objects. A childish and girly, pink game console and a metal toy gymnast perhaps continuing the theme of performance and athleticism. Benigno pushes the gymnast around just as he will later push Alicia around. The toy appears to have a switch on it to make it move. Like the toy, Alicia is later switched off; inert, inanimate and manhandled by Benigno. The shelf also has a hair clip on it which Benigno takes. The hair clip has later significance in the prison sequence as it is one of the few possessions Benigno has with him and which he is buried with. The clip is an interesting object for Almodóvar to decide upon. The object is intimate but innocent in that it is used on Alicia's body yet

Fig. 3

has no erotic significance. Had Benigno stolen Alicia's underwear, the audience would likely be repulsed and unable to sympathise with him for the rest of the film.

The next significant image of the sequence focuses on setting and costume. As Benigno leaves the room he bumps into Alicia who has just come out of the shower; she screams. Her orange dressing gown continues the warm colour palette associated with her character. The semi opaque glass wall behind her is also interesting (Fig. 4). Glass and mirrors are used frequently in this and other Almodóvar films. In this setting it could be used to make a point about Benigno's invasion of privacy and unfulfilled voyeurism; Benigno's desire to look but not being able to. Glass is important for Benigno and Alicia who are initially separated by glass; the large glass windows of the dance studio just as later Benigno is separated from Marco and Alicia behind glass in the prison.

Paintings and Books

Often in films when one analyses paintings, books, objects that are in the back ground and not imperative to the plot, one runs the risk of reading too much into things, however, in the case of Almodóvar, such analysis can prove interesting. Almodóvar describes the obsessive detail that he

Fig. 4

puts into his *mise-en-scène*: '*...when I'm making a movie its necessary to surround myself with lots of images that have a lot of meaning for me and to the story.*'[5]

A.O. Scott comments upon this by saying that Almodóvar's *mise-en-scène* is:

> Saturated with meaning and thick with feeling beyond what the viewer is able to analyse or the film-maker to explain.[6]

A mid-shot as Benigno enters Dr Roncero's office denotes him looking towards a surrealist painting perhaps in the style of Rene Magritte. The painting seems to consist of mannequins with bicycle wheels and what seem to be lenses or magnifying glasses. The painting helps to establish and foreshadow some of the themes within the film. The female form is fragmented, headless and thus unable to communicate; reduced to an object (Fig. 5).

Books are also important both symbolically and intertextually. When in the clinic, a book is shown in **shallow focus** with the title and author in focus. *The Night of the Hunter* is a 1953 book, later adapted into a film in 1955. The half-read book is a disrupted narrative just as the narrative of Alicia's life has been disrupted by her coma. The book is based on the real life serial killer Harry Powers who ensnared his victims using Lonely Hearts ads. The book is a gothic thriller set during the depression era in which

Fig. 5

Harry Powell, an ex-convict, persuades a mother of two to marry him in the hopes that he will be able to find her ex-husband's money. He ends up murdering the mother and then hunting the children. Whilst one cannot draw a direct comparison between Benigno and the far more sinister and murderous Harry Powell, the inclusion of the book suggests a few things. Before Alicia's coma and subsequent rape and awakening she was reading about a violent serial killer, but never got to the conclusion of the story to see Powell convicted for his crimes, just as she will not know what happened to the criminal that abused her. Secondly, the title *Night of the Hunter* might also refer to the turning point in the film; the 'night' when Benigno rapes Alicia. Viewing it with this intertextual reference makes the rape seem altogether more sinister than it appears on first viewing.

The second book which is focused upon is *The Hours* (1998) by Michael Cunningham, which was also later adapted into a film. The book is seen on Benigno's bedside table. *The Hours* is a Pulitzer Prize-winning novel about three generations of women affected by a Virginia Wolf novel. Like *Talk to Her*, *The Hours* plays with chronology, deals with issues of mental health and explores the beauty that can be found in the mundane. Almodóvar draws the connection in his *mise-en-scène* between water and death to that in *The Hours*.

On the cover you see a detail of a painting of a body underwater, with her hand resting on the water [...] on one hand it is a confession that

I love *The Hours*, I would have liked to have made that movie but they already did it. But it is also about the theme of death and water' referring to the fact that Alicia enters a coma on a rainy day and Benigno commits suicide on a rainy day.[7]

Mise-en-scène and Framing

There are several points within the film where barriers, both real and symbolic, are put between characters, and points where character's bodies create frames and shapes within the image, in the tradition of classical painting.

The rule of thirds is a theory in painting and photography where the frame is split into nine parts by two sets of intersecting lines. Where the lines meet are points which the eye is naturally drawn to. Therefore, when significant objects are placed within these areas the spectator focuses on them. The rule of thirds can be applied to a shot in *Talk to Her* where Alicia is having her hair cut (Fig. 6). Benigno's body forms one of the vertical axis of the rule of thirds grid. Rosa's arm, holding Alicia's head, follows the bottom horizontal line and Rosa's body creates the other vertical line. Alicia's head is at one of the intersections and thus, despite the fact that Benigno and Rosa are the ones who are actively having a conversation, the spectator naturally focuses in on Alicia. The framing makes us complicit with Benigno in watching Alicia.

Fig. 6

Almodóvar uses vertical and horizontal lines found naturally within the sets in order to make meaning. For example, many of the shots in Lydia's room are filmed from outside the room looking in. The window and door frames create a symbolic barrier which separates Marco from Lydia (Fig. 7). Although present in the room, Marco never enters the 'symbolic room' created by the barrier. El Niño, Benigno and the nurses all enter this part of the frame but, just as Marco is unable to talk to Lydia, so too he is unable to occupy the same space as her. Lydia's body is also fragmented by the window frame just as it is fragmented during the earlier dressing scene. Her head is in a different part of the frame to her body perhaps symbolic of the fact that whilst her body is still working her mind is not.

Fig. 7

References

1. Almodóvar, Pedro. Self- Interview www.sonyclassics.com/talktoher/flashwebsite/core/hasFlash.html(accessed 03/08/2014)

2. Almodóvar, Pedro. Self-Interview

3. Almodóvar, Pedro. Self-Interview

4. Mercer, John and Shingler, Martin. (2004) *Melodrama, Genre, Style, Sensibility*. London: Wallflower Press. p. 76

5. Almodóvar, Pedro interviewed by Scott, A. O in Paula Willoquet-Maricondi. (2004) *Pedro Almodóvar: Interviews*. USA University Press of Mississippi. p. 167

6. Scott, p. 167

7. Almodóvar, Pedro. Self-Interview

Gender

In 1949 existentialist and feminist Philosopher Simone De Beauvoir wrote in her book *The Second Sex*: 'One is not born, but rather becomes, a woman', separating gender into two categories; the biological and the acquired gender characteristics.[1] This concept is arguably central for *Talk to Her* which plays with the idea of gender being a fixed attribute and sees gender instead as something flexible and fluid.

Gender roles in *Talk to Her* are arguably represented as a socially constructed rather than innately determined with characters in careers typically assigned to the opposite gender. Lydia is a female bull fighter in a typically chauvinist industry and Benigno is a male nurse in a very female heavy environment. Unlike the more obvious gender bending in *All About My Mother* with transsexual and transvestite characters in a state of physical and visual gender transition or, the really obvious forced sex change operation in *The Skin I Live In*, the gender transitioning in *Talk to Her* is more subtle with D' Lugo referring to it as '*shuffling of characters in which the conventional boundaries that define their identities and stories are blurred and weakened.*'[2]

Almodóvar's blurring of the strict rigid definitions of masculinity and femininity can be viewed as postmodernist. Postmodernism is a concept that arose in the 1960s, in a simple sense, a postmodernist work is one that is typified by a mixing of styles and a breakdown of conventional rules and structures.

Building on postmodernist theory and De Beauvoir's work, in the late 1980s Judith Butler developed her theory of Gender Performativity, the idea that gender characteristics are established and endure through continual performance of gendered behaviour and appearances. She says: 'gender is not a fact, the various acts of gender create the idea of gender, and without these acts there would be no gender at all'.[3] Butler goes on to say that there is a 'tacit, collective agreement to perform, produce and sustain discrete and polar genders as cultural fictions'.[4] Gender performativity is interesting to consider in relation to Almodóvar's body of films as a whole in its most obvious form with men performing female gender characteristics in the form of drag queens such as Letal in *High Heels*. In *Talk to Her* Lydia, Marco and Benigno can be seen to *perform* both male and female gender characteristics at different times.

Masculinity

During the sequence on the balcony Katerina speaks about a new ballet which she plans to choreograph about World War One.

KATERINA: There's Ballerinas also in the ballet. When a soldier dies, from his body emerges his soul, his ghost and that's a ballerina. Long tutus like the 'Willis' in Giselle, classical, but with blood stain red.

BENIGNO: That's lovely. Alicia's loving it.

KATERINA: Yes. From death emerges life, from the male emerges the female.

The implication here could be that at their core, the men in *Talk to Her* have innately feminine qualities and that, applying Judith Butler's idea of Gender Performativity, the men are merely *performing* their masculinity. Secondly, like the Ballet, in *Talk to Her*, Alicia is granted life at the expense of a male death, the death of her unborn son, and granted a future at the expense of Benigno's death so there is perhaps a message here about male sacrifice. Perhaps, Franco's death could be seen as a sacrifice that allows women in Spain more freedom.

Benigno's name means harmless/ benign and Javier Cámara's performance helps to illustrate this typically feminine quality. Throughout the film, Benigno is softly spoken, physically chubby and spends most of the film with a wide eyed expression of hope and innocence. Benigno is effeminate and caring with knowledge of hair dressing and make up. Marco by contrast has a much more traditionally masculine, muscular physique and, had we not seen his sensitivity demonstrated in the opening scene, one might be lead to believe that he is meant to adhere to a more macho archetype. Almodóvar won't let us get away that easily though. Marco is both masculine and sensitive, moved to tears by dance, music and the memories that they evoke.

Suzie Mackenzie notes that 'Men in Almodóvar's films are frequently defeated by [...] emasculation'[5] she puts this in the context of Spain and Franco's dictatorship and how the community Almodóvar grew up with was filled with strong women and absent men. Strangely in *Talk to Her* the two characters appear to become more masculine as the film progresses. Benigno can be said to have been emasculated by his mother but, develops his masculine character traits in the typically masculine setting of the prison; he has a beard and speaks in a much more forceful urgent tone than his earlier chirpy and campy performances at the hospital. The idea that one can *become* more masculine fits with De Beauvoir's ideas on gender as a fluid concept.

Marco and Benigno's Relationship

Marco and Benigno are brought together by coincidence and their relationship follows a cyclical pattern through the film. They are first in close proximity at the theatre at Café Müller and are framed in close up (Fig. 1). Just as, later in the film, Benigno watches the unaware Alicia, Marco is not aware of Benigno's gaze. For Benigno, the close framing could be interpreted as an intimate moment between two people; however, for Marco, the moment is purely individual. The importance of this moment for each character is made prominent again later where the two meet at the hospital. Whilst Benigno remembers Marco clearly and states 'I know you', Marco has no recollection of Benigno. Benigno proceeds to whisper to Alicia 'I told you about him, he cried watching Café Müller'. Rather than seeming disturbed by the weight that Benigno seems to have put on this chance encounter, Marco's face is instead filled with sadness as he stares at Alicia. Whilst Benigno's performance is chirpy and light, Marco seems deep and emotional but about what it is not clear; he is an enigma.

Fig. 1

Framing is of further importance during the first prison scene. The men speak through a pane of glass in a **shot/reverse shot** sequence, the glass reminiscent of their simultaneous unity and isolation. The two are then filmed in an impossible shot, the camera panning as if through the side of the glass wall, perhaps suggesting that their friendship can surpass the vast divisions between them. Marco's reflection appears on the glass as if superimposing Benigno and then vice versa (Fig. 2). During this conversation Benigno describes how he reads Marco's travel books at night and states, 'It was like travelling for months with you at my side'. This is the first implication that Marco will begin to walk as if in Benigno's path for the rest of the film. In the next scene this is made explicit. Marco, now living in Benigno's apartment draws back the curtain on the balcony and to his amazement and then enthral, sees Alicia enter the dance studio. Like Benigno, Marco takes on the role of peeping tom, a voyeur looking at the dancers and then upon Alicia without her consent or knowledge. This gaze is made all the more explicit by the fact that the camera cuts from the naturalistic longshot point-of-view to a close up of Alicia filmed from within the room. Emphasising what cannot be seen but is felt by Marco. Marco quickly shuts the door and turns to see the large picture of Alicia in her coma that sits above Benigno's bed. Like Benigno, Marco cannot look away and breathes quickly as if filled with emotion.

Fig. 2

The film ends as it begins with a chance encounter at a dance performance where, in another coincidence; Marco and Alicia meet. The **non-diegetic title** Marco y Alicia reminds the audience of the previous titles 'Benigno y Alicia' and 'Marco y Lydia'. It could be interpreted that Marco and Alicia are about to engage in a romantic relationship, however one could equally interpret this as being part of Marco further following in Benigno's footsteps. Between Marco and Alicia is an empty chair, simultaneously symbolising the loss of Benigno but equally, Benigno's death has quite literally cleared the way for Marco to begin a relationship with Alicia.

Male Friendship

In most of Almodóvar's films men are secondary characters and in some, such as *Bad Habits*, they appear as wall paper; reduced to *mise-en-scène* rather than given focus. Thomas Sotinel identifies that Marco and Benigno's relationship is a departure from this tradition 'for once men occupy all the space [...] not tearing each other apart but offering mutual comfort.'[6]

In a telephone scene which cross cuts between the prison and the outside of the clinic, Marco and Benigno solidify their friendship. Marco has just found out about Benigno's crime and conviction and is called by Benigno. He asks 'How could you do that, Benigno?' but this is the only chastisement that Benigno receives from Marco. Benigno asks 'Hey man, are you still my friend?' Their conversation adheres to stereotypes of male friendship, it is devoid of sentiment and focuses on practicalities; in this case finding out what happened to Alicia.

As the film progresses, the power dynamic shifts in their friendship. At points in the film Benigno gives advice conforming to the role of 'care giver' or 'agony aunt'. He implores Marco to talk to Lydia:

BENIGNO: You have to pay attention to women, talk to them. Be thoughtful occasionally. Caress them. Remember they exist, they are alive, they matter to us.

Whereas, at other points Benigno takes on a dominant role. He says he likes the idea of Marco being his tenant and gives him orders such as '... and get me another lawyer', to which Marco unquestioningly agrees.

It could be argued that there are homosexual undertones to Marco and Benigno's friendship. An example of this occurs during the first prison scene. Benigno says 'I've been thinking about you a lot, especially at night' the camera then quickly cuts back to Marco whose raised eyebrowed facial expression suggests he is disturbed by Benigno's comment. Conversely, in the second prison scene Marco doesn't mind Benigno's affections. Benigno says, 'I'd like to be able to hug you, but I'd have to ask for a vis a vis' this time Marco isn't bothered by the fact they might be interpreted as romantic lovers. Towards the end of the film, just before Benigno commits suicide, the camera pans across Benigno's desk and dwells upon objects important to his life. A voiceover accompanies the scene where Benigno reads out his suicide note. In it he says that Marco is his only friend.

Fathers

In *Talk to Her* masculinity could be seen as an attribute that is inherited from fathers. Absent fathers are a reoccurring theme in Almodóvar's work in such films at *Matador* (1986), *Law of Desire* and *All About My Mother*. In *Talk to Her*, Benigno's father is physically absent and so is his memory and image. It is implied that his lack of fatherly influence is the reason why he opted for more feminine pastimes such a hair dressing and learning beauty treatments.

When fathers are present in Almodóvar's films they are more often than not psychotic in the case of Nicholas the murderous step father in *Kika* (1993) or Antonio Banderas's character Robert in *The Skin I Live In* (who performs a sex change on the man whom he accuses of molesting his daughter). Fathers are sometimes sexually aggressive and perverted in the case of the laundrette owner in *Labyrinth of Passion* who has sex with his own daughter. More often than not fathers and step fathers are dead, a possible metaphor for the death of Franco. Equally, fathers are often killed off. The perpetrators are often the desperate women in their lives as is the case in *What Have I Done to Deserve This?* (1984), *High Heels* and *Volver*. Almodóvar's problematic stance on fathers continues in *Talk to Her*, as we know, Benigno's own father has abandoned him and started a new life in Sweden. The other father within the film, Alicia's father Dr Roncero, has what, we might assume from the few scenes we are presented with, to have a fairly practical relationship with his daughter. He is clearly wealthy and has seemingly spared no expense in hiring two nurses to look after Alicia day and night. He is able to provide for Alicia into adulthood and, we assume, pays for her dance tuition. However, we never see Alicia and her father actually having a conversation at any point in the film, nor is he much of a presence at the hospital. This could imply that communication between the genders is a father daughter issue as well as a romantic issue.

The other father that is spoken about but not seen is Lydia's father. He too seems to have had a dysfunctional relationship with Lydia whom he wished was a boy and named Lydia (coming from the word Lidia literally means the art of bullfighting) which, as Marco comments, sealed her fate. Almodóvar's own father was a present feature within his life first making a living as a mule driver and then owning a gas station. Like Lydia's father, Almodóvar's father had specific expectations for him and sent him away from a young age to train to be a priest. Suzie Mackenzie suggests that the film as a whole is a 'Hymn and a homage to Antonio [Almodóvar's father] to the father who didn't speak much' who didn't understand his son but 'whom, assuredly, he loved.'[7]

Almodóvar's negative portrayal of father figures may come from witnessing the abuse of some of his fellow classmates by members of the priesthood. Alternatively the corrupt or ineffective father could be understood in the context of Spain's history with the father figure symbolic of the patriarchal power of the Franco regime.

Marco as Father, Benigno as Child

To a certain extent, Marco and Benigno's relationship can be seen as a coded version of a father-child relationship particularly through the use of *mise-en-scène* and performance. Marco is physically larger and taller than Benigno. He seems older than Benigno both in his mannerisms and appearance.[8] He is balding and wears suit jackets as opposed to Benigno's full head of hair (which is actually a convincing wig as Javier Cámara is bald!) and medical scrubs with big white buttons which give him the appearance of perpetually looking like a little boy in pyjamas.

During one particular scene outside the hospital they are momentarily thrust out of the role of friends and into a father son relationship. The scene begins in the hospital café where Marco meets Benigno who is eating. Like a child, Benigno has a glass of milk with his meal and is dipping his food in it. The shot is filmed from over Marco's shoulder making Benigno look even smaller than him. Like a father who has returned from holiday, Marco has brought Benigno gifts; travel books for him and Alicia to read. Benigno asks for a lift home. At the car, Benigno tells Marco that he wants to marry Alicia. Marco is outraged and, like a parent talking to a naughty child, he snaps at Benigno: 'Get in the car!' Then, again like a father he proceeds to lecture Benigno about how inappropriate his intentions are. At the end of his rant he shakes his head and tuts exasperatedly whilst Benigno sulks and looks out the window like a misunderstood teenager.

C.D.C Reeve comments upon the 'transformative power of film' and how, by the act of rape (and in doing so losing his virginity) Benigno symbolically achieves puberty: 'It's as if he has become an adolescent male overnight.'[9] From having the chubby, fresh faced demeanour of a small boy at the hospital, when we see him at the prison he is bearded and slimmer. Like a teenager he seems unable to control his emotions and becomes melodramatic saying, 'If this goes on I am capable of anything! They say I am a psychopath? Well then I'll behave like one!'

Furthermore, later, like a teenager not quite ready for manhood, he wishes for affection from his 'parent' in the form of hugs. Like a parent, Marco's 'love' for his coded 'son' is unconditional. Even after Dr Vega has told him about the rape he still stands by his 'child'. C.D.C Reeve also goes on to comment that Benigno's 'facial appearance [brings him] closer to that of the swarthy Marco'.[10] Whilst Reeve's point is that the two characters are merging closer together, one could also interpret this in a father/ son context; as sons grow older they inherit the genetics of masculinity from their fathers.

Crying

Almodóvar said of crying in the film 'I would have liked to call it 'The Man Who Cried' had it not been the existing title of a Sally Potter film'[11] which puts an interesting focus on Marco's tears; crying being typically viewed as an effeminate quality. He goes on to say 'one of the ideas that I wanted to convey was a man who cried for emotional reasons linked to a work of art- from seeing a work of enormous beauty'.[12] Marco cries at four points in the film, first during Café Müller, second when killing the snake, thirdly when he sees the Spanish Guitar and lastly when Benigno dies. Often he cries when exposed to art, but he also cries for his flawed friend. Almodóvar says:

> I think Cocteau said that beauty can be painful. I suppose that he meant the beauty of the people, I think that the situations which bring unexpected and extraordinary moments of beauty can bring out tears, tears of pain more than pleasure.[13]

The audience and Marco can find a certain beauty in Benigno. Despite his role as a rapist, he is endearing. Marco and arguably the audience, feel sympathy for him even after knowing what he has done. There is a certain flawed beauty in Benigno's unwavering conviction that he and Alicia are in love that seems to touch Marco.

It is interesting that Benigno who is the more obviously sensitive of the two men does not cry, perhaps implying he is less able to connect with art something that is emphasised in his conversation with Katerina when he proves poor at analysing meaning from her proposed choreography.

Performers and Passive Bodies

Alicia and Lydia both use their bodies for their career; Alicia as a dancer (a typically feminine role) and Lydia as a Matador (a typical masculine role). Yet, both characters end up in the same situation, as passive objects unable to move or think for themselves.

In addition to being active, Alicia and Lydia are both performers who perform in front of large crowds at the bull-fighting arena and dance theatres. Like Benigno with Alicia, Marco is first attracted to Lydia when she is active and performing however, unlike Benigno whose passion for Alicia seems to increase she is passive, Marco is repulsed by her passivity and says, 'I don't recognise her body'.

The idea of these women as performers is reinforced through the casting as both actresses are singers. Leonore Watling (Alicia) is a singer in a band called Marlango whilst Rosario Flores (Lydia) is a successful Latin Music singer who would be well known by Spanish and Latin American audiences. Rosario Flores's music videos often highlight her femininity and sexuality. She is very obviously and willingly objectified; often wearing tight revealing clothing or lingerie. Like Lydia's role as a Matador, Rosario Flores is keen to celebrate the iconography of Spain in her career in videos such as *Tu Boca* (2014) where she dresses in a traditional red flamenco dress.

For most of the film Alicia's body is inert. This is highlighted in many shots particularly in the frequent **bird's-eye view** shots of her body and breasts which are fragmented from the rest of her body by tight camera framing. Her passivity is most notable in the opening scene, some of which is shot from between Alicia's raised knees in which we see Benigno and another nurse washing her vagina (Fig. 3). The scene takes on a comical edge through the crude squirting of liquids and vigorous scrubbing.

Fig. 3

Lydia's passivity is somewhat foreshadowed in the sequence of being dressed into her Matadora costume the Traje de Luces; a colloquial term literally translated as the suit of lights due to its extensive use of gold and silver threads and sequins. Filmed mainly in close up and extreme close up, the highly colourful and intricate designs of the Traje de Luces are examined and celebrated as is Lydia's passive body. As with Alicia's body in the early scenes at the hospital, Lydia's body is fragmented. Firstly the camera focuses in on a foot and leg filmed in close up as her assistant pulls on her pink tights (known as the Taleguilla) just as Alicia's feet have been fragmented in the previous scene (Fig. 4). Next her waistline is shot in close up as the assistant pulls up her trousers. Her stomach has obvious scars on it emphasising her fragility and role as a performer whose body is put on the line for their art. As with Alicia in the hospital,

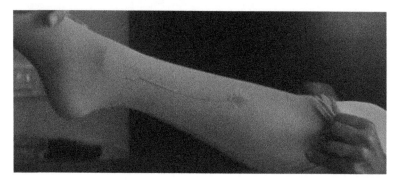

Fig. 4

Lydia is being cared for by a man who takes on the active role within the scene; in this case an unimportant and unnamed aid. Just as Alicia and later Lydia needs skilled and intimate care, Lydia's dressing seems to require expert skill. An extreme close up of a tool hooking a button into its button hole cuts to a long shot of Lydia's jacket being pulled on and then vigorously pulled into place by the male aid.

Peter Bradshaw describes the scene as being 'like the robing of a priest before mass'.[14] Like the Catholic Church, bullfighting in Spain is filled with ritual and tradition and, despite its controversial status amongst animal rights activists, is viewed as an important part of Spanish cultural identity. This particular scene seems to fit with what Robert B. Pippin describes as the 'complexities of exhibition, of gesture, dress, costume and display' the difficulty, he suggests, amongst all of the colour and sparkle of costume and the complexities of performance, is in actually knowing who anyone is.[15] Lydia is performing a role that many others have played, following sporting protocol and cultural traditions. The theme of 'performance' is heightened by the red curtain behind her, a pervasive symbol from the start of the film of drama and theatricality.

In a shot that echoes the penultimate dance sequence, after Lydia is gored, a bird's-eye view tracking shot denotes her now passive, limp and fragile body being taken from the bull fighting arena by several men (Fig. 5). Marco, like the male dancer in Café Müller, can be seen at the edge of the frame franticly clearing a path for her. In an interesting gender reversal, a goring scene in the 2012 Spanish, Pablo Berger film

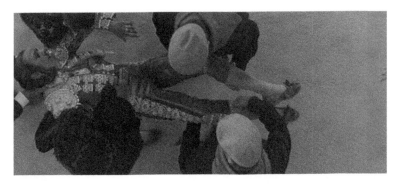

Fig. 5

Blancanieves is shot almost identically to that in *Talk to Her* but with a male bullfighter instead of a female one. The Matador in *Blancanieves* is paralysed by the goring and becomes passive and emasculated, subservient to his wife (a wicked stepmother archetype).

In a wider sense, the passivity of the females could be seen to act as a metaphor for Spain as a whole under the rule of Franco or as a comment the passive roles that women were forced into. Looking at it in this sense, Lydia's Matador outfit can be symbolic of the forceful imposition of tradition and prescribed Spanish identity under the dictator's rule.

Chauvinism

Another gender issue the film raises is that of chauvinism within the bull-fighting world and as a consequence, in Spanish society. Although in the 19th Century female bullfighters were allowed, under Franco's dictatorship they were only permitted to ride on horses in the arena. As a consequence, women have consistently struggled to enter this male dominated world. For the character of Lydia, Almodóvar may have been influenced by the career of Cristina Sanchez, Spain's most successful Matadora of the late 90's who quit in 1999 due to the sexism she allegedly faced. In an article in The Guardian Newspaper she is reported to have said: 'Bullfighting is a man's world, geared to male psychology and needs. I've got further than any woman before me and I'm very proud of that.'[16] The bull in Spain is often symbolic of a man and as Sanchez said:

Bulls are associated with courage and virility and some men cannot forgive a woman for being able to hold her own in that environment [...] I realised prejudice had won when I wasn't accepted in any of the top festivals this year and I refuse to accept a life trailing around second-rate rings fighting dud bulls.[17]

The film's message here could be interpreted in two ways, firstly in opposition to the chauvinism of Spanish culture by depicting Lydia as a successful Matadora. However, equally the film could be taken as an acceptance of chauvinism; after all, Lydia is killed by the *male* bull.

Lydia: Adhering to and Challenging Feminine Stereotypes

Talk to Her is impossible to consider in terms of strict **binary opposites** as characters like Lydia both adhere to and subvert gender stereotypes. Lydia has followed in her father's footsteps in her choice of career in the highly patriarchal world of Bull Fighting. Lydia's slim and boyish physicality adds to her **androgyny** when in her bull fighting costume, yet later, when dressed for socialising, she is attractive and feminine wearing a low cut, tight fitting, floral dress. Lydia is a paradox, someone who is simultaneously strong but weak, active yet passive, feminine yet masculine and desperate yet stable.

Lydia's costume, hair and make-up throughout the film alters how masculine or feminine she can be interpreted as being. When Lydia is in her bull fighting outfit with her hair scraped back all aspects of traditional femininity are erased, she appears boyish despite the fact her outfit is a baby pink in colour. Her facial expression, a determined frown, and her strong self-assured posture align her with stereotypically masculine attributes.

Although Lydia denies it, for much of the film she appears desperate, a quality of the damsel in distress role played by many women in Hollywood Cinema. Lydia appears on a TV chat show and has a cat fight with the host of the show. The set is lurid green sixties style wallpaper which clashes with the ginger hair of the chat show host. Lydia wears a skimpy tight black dress and knee high boots with her hair loose and curly. The camera focuses mainly on her face to show her clearly disapproving expressions to the chat show hosts insistence on bringing up El Niño de Valencia (her ex-lover). Body language is particularly important in this scene. The host of the show initially touches Lydia on the arms in a caring way whilst she says to her 'Talking about your problems is the first step to overcoming them'. Her body language becomes more and more cloying as she grabs Lydia and drags her back to her seat. Lydia finally struggles to get away leaving the host to fall off the sofa looking dishevelled. Their struggle mirrors many of Lydia's other struggles- with El Niño de Valencia, her struggle to communicate and eventually her struggle with the bull.

The next time we see Lydia is in the bull fighting ring, still struggling but now much more in control. The scene is shot in slow motion with the focus shifting from the bull to Lydia's determined face to her male spectators Marco, who looks upon with awe, and El Niño de Valencia and his manager who seem concerned. All **diegetic sounds** have been removed from the shots with Lydia in them and the **non-diegetic sound** of a traditional slow Spanish ballad plays. The song, combined with the slow motion, helps to draw a connection between Lydia and the bull. The bull could represent Lydia's masculinity and aggression and how she tames these qualities. Alternatively the bull could represent the men in Lydia's life who she struggles to have relationships with. The scene is not dissimilar to the opening dance sequence where female dancers run towards each other and the male dancers try to clear a path. Lydia attempts to coerce the bull to move in a particular direction so the two don't collide. The final shot in the ring is taken from a low angle. Lydia looks triumphant, the scene is shot in shallow focus with a blurred crowd in the background cheering. The scene then cuts to an old black and white photograph of a man who looks similar to Lydia with most of his body in a cast; perhaps her father. One might get the sense that Lydia's motivation might be to prove herself to her father in a masculine sport.

The scene then cuts to a bar, Lydia's femininity is much more evident, unlike the slicked back braid in the arena, her hair is now loose and curly, she wears a tight dress which shows off her curves. She meets Marco for the first time in the bar. The scene might sound like the start of a normal romance, 'a man and woman meet in a bar', but the scene is unromantic. Marco's intentions are to get an interview whilst Lydia's intentions are to get away from El Niño de Valencia and potentially make him jealous in the process. Lydia continues to demonstrate typically feminine traits is during the following scene when Marco drives her home. She goes into her house and runs out screaming afraid of a snake that lies within. Lydia's performance in this scene errs towards the melodramatic, screaming, kissing her necklace, and rubbing herself frantically as if the snake has made her dirty; she epitomises the stereotype of 'the hysterical woman'. For a moment, the film adheres to traditional gender stereotypes. Marco enters the house and kills the snake in an act of macho heroism whilst Lydia sits in the car and waits for rescue. Marco is shot from behind in a medium long shot, his body obscures the act of killing just as with the later rape of Alicia, the audience are spared from witnessing violence and force. Marco's performance during the kill is swift and matter of fact. This brief interlude of strict binary opposites is quickly broken as Marco begins to cry and gets a tissue from his pocket to wipe away his tears. The next shot is a point-of-view shot in the car wing mirror as Lydia, now calm, watches Marco exiting the house and observes his tears. The power dynamic shifts again as Lydia abruptly orders Marco 'Take me to a hotel'. Marco doesn't look at Lydia during their conversation and follows orders obediently. Lydia is back in control with Marco reduced to chauffeur.

Absent Mothers

In a film that is mainly about men, the absence of mothers is notable. Benigno's mother, whom he describes as 'not ill but lazy', is never seen but helps us to understand why Benigno may feel at home with passive women as he takes on the role of carer twice in his lifetime both as carer to his mother and then carer to Alicia. Alicia, who has no mother, is mothered by her dance teacher Katerina who talks on a maternal and protective role throughout.

Visibly older, Katerina seems to have taken a special interest in Alicia and, like Benigno, a special interest in Alicia's body. In the first shot we see of her in the dance studio she is gently correcting Alicia's posture just as later she will make Alicia do extra leg lifts even though as Alicia says in a weary voice 'I've done 100 today already'. Katerina is also maternally protective of Alicia as can be seen in the last scene at the theatre. Katerina glances over to Alicia and beams with pride. Her expression is replaced with horror and fear when she realises that she is talking to Marco. In a motherly way, she ushers Alicia back to her seat with her arms around her saying 'come, come'. Katerina quite literally shares the same place for Alicia as her own parents as is evident through the *mise-en-scène* and the small framed photographs on Alicia's bedside one of Katerina and one of her parents when they were younger.

In an odd way, Benigno can be thought of as a mother figure. Muñoz states that Benigno's care of Alicia is motherly and 'includes "maternal" feminised activities such as bathing her, dressing her, fixing her hair...'.[18] In addition to this, storytelling could be seen as a maternal activity in the way mothers tell stories to children before they go to bed. Later, Benigno mothers Marco, urging him to take some hot honey; the kind of home remedy a mother might make for a sick infant.

Sexuality

It is generally problematic to link sexuality to masculinity/ femininity as one can be homosexual but adhere to masculine/ feminine stereotypes whilst equally one could be heterosexual but be considered effeminate or butch. For the beginning half of the film Benigno could be interpreted as asexual as his love for Alicia is platonic and maternal and, we assume, that at this point he has not acted inappropriately with Alicia's body. When Dr Roncero visits Alicia he notices that Benigno is rubbing Alicia's inner thigh and, disturbed, asks him what his sexual orientation is. Annoyed by the question Benigno replies 'Men' which seems to satisfy him. Thus, homosexuality is coded as being safe whereas heterosexuality is coded as being a threat.

In his blog Culture Court Lawrence Russell describes Lydia as being 'really a bisexual foil' who 'can be viewed as a fantasy figure for straights and gays alike'.[19] Due to the way in which she can be considered attractive both when dressed and behaving in a feminine way and in the masculine world of the bull fighting ring.

References

1. De Beauvoir, Simone (1949) *The Second Sex*. Paris: Editions Galimard. p. 293

2. D'Lugo, Marvin. (2006) *Contemporary Film-makers: Pedro Almodóvar*. USA: University of Illinois Press. p. 109

3. Butler, Judith. (Dec., 1988) *Performative Acts and Gender Constitution: An Essay in Phenomenology and Feminist Theory* Theatre Journal, Vol. 40, No. 4. p. 524

4. Butler, p. 524

5. Mackenzie, Suzie in Paula Willoquet-Maricondi. (2004) *Pedro Almodóvar: Interviews.* USA University Press of Mississippi. pp. 155-156

6. Sotinel, Thomas. (2010) *Masters of Cinema: Pedro Almodóvar.* Paris: Cahiers Du Cinema Sarl. p. 32

7. Mackenzie, p. 158

8. We assume that Benigno is 24

9. Reeve, C.D.C in Eaton, A.W (2009) *Philosophers on Film: Talk to Her.* Oxon: Routledge. p. 100

10. Reeve, p. 100

11. Almodóvar interviewed by Scott, A.O in Paula Willoquet-Maricondi. (2004) *Pedro Almodóvar: Interviews.* USA University Press of Mississippi. p. 163

12. Scott, p. 163

13. Almodóvar, Pedro. (2002) Self-Interview www.sonyclassics.com/talktoher/flashwebsite/core/hasFlash.html

14. Bradshaw, Peter. (Friday 23rd August 2002) *Talk to Her* www.theguardian.com/film/2002/aug/23/1 (accessed 19/09/14)

15. Pippin, B. Robert in Eaton, A.W (2009) *Philosophers on Film: Talk to Her.* Oxon: Routledge. p. 33

16. Chritina Sanchez, quoted in Adela Gooch Saturday 22 May 1999 Bullfighter gored by male rivals www.theguardian.com/world/1999/may/22/1 (accessed 25/09/14)

17. Sanchez, ibid.

18. Acevedo-Muñoz, Ernesto R. (2007) *Pedro Almodóvar.* London: British Film Institute. p. 251

19. Russell, Lawrence. www.culturecourt.com/F/Latin/TalkToHer.htm (accessed 25/09/14)

Physicality and The Body

Male physicality is important in many of Almodóvar's films and the male body is often objectified. In the fake film within the film *Tie me Up! Tie me Down!* a gladiator, with an Adonis-like body, stands bare-chested in a masked metal motorbike helmet, in the middle of the frame, unwilling to show his disfigured face. In *Matador* the male form is similarly objectified. Almodóvar depicts young bull fighters training in tight leggings and sportswear. The camera focuses in on the young men's buttocks and crotch in an **eye-line match** sequence from the point of view of a detective. Similarly, the opening sequence of *Labyrinth of Passion* is a set of eye-line matches of men's crotches. Whilst *Talk to Her* does not celebrate or objectify the bodies of its central male protagonists so brazenly, before the guitar sequence there is a seemingly out of place shot of a beautiful male body (Fig. 1). The mystery man is filmed in a bird's-eye view shot and swims a length of the pool before emerging; smiling in a close up. Cynthia Freeland suggests that the purpose of the shot is 'to conjure up emotions of sensuous pleasure and exploration of bodily rhythms'.[1] Perhaps in a film with so many female bodies it is a moment to appreciate the male form.

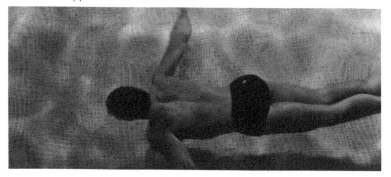

Fig. 1

The physicality of female actors is important within *Talk to Her*. Both Alicia and Lydia use their bodies for professions which require skill and athleticism. In preparing for their roles, Leonor Watling (Alicia) and Rosario Flores (Lydia) had to practice yoga in order to relax their bodies to give a realistic performance whilst in a coma.

In order to achieve the self control which allows one to disconnect from the exterior world, Leonor and Rosario took yoga classes (Yyengar, to be specific) for three months before the shoot. I wanted them to be sunk within the very depth of their beings, an unfathomable depth, and for that they had to be very relaxed.[2]

The film explores different types of male and female bodies. Alicia's body is pale, soft and fleshy, described by Freeland as being 'odalisque like' likening it to nude paintings of Turkish concubines in the nineteenth century (Fig. 2).[3] Such paintings, like Benigno and Marco's gaze, celebrate the curves of the female body.

Fig. 2: 'Odalisque' painted by Jules Joseph Lefebvre (1874).

Lydia's body by contrast is more muscular, tanned and angular. Freeland says:

Hers is a different sort of beauty from Alicia's. Rather than being modern and young, Lydia has the narrow profile, large nose, strong brows, and dark staring eyes of an ancient Iberian queen like the sculptures that inspired Picasso to create several of the women in his revolutionary painting Les Demoiselles d' Avingnon.[4]

Just as Benigno's chubby physicality and height don't quite fit the traditional role of male romantic lead, so too Piña Bausch's choreography includes different kinds of bodies than one would expect to see in contemporary dance. At the age of sixty-two her own scantily clad body is exhibited within the opening dance sequence. Her body is both muscular and lean but aging and veined. Combined with her limp hair, closed eyes and staggering movement, she exudes an air of frailty.

The body is also seen as an important motif within the film. The unconscious body is represented in different ways; as a landscape, as a doll, as a corpse, as a fairy tale princess.

Fig. 3: 'Les Demoiselles d' Avingnon', Pablo Picasso (1907).

The Medicalised Body

Alicia's often naked body is often represented in a medicalised, matter of fact way. This is exemplified in the scene where Rosa, who notices that Alicia has missed her period and is swollen, presses her stomach and breasts robustly looking for signs of infection (Fig. 4). There are several of long shot bird's-eye views of Alicia, taking in her whole body. She is objectified, but rather than sexualising the naked female form, Alicia's motionless poses make her seem almost like a corpse in a mortuary.

Fig. 4

In another example, a bird's-eye view, closer in than that previously mentioned, sees Alicia's breasts centred in the middle of the frame.

Benigno and the other nurse's hands scrub vigorously. The shot then jump cuts to Alicia's feet, which are again being cleaned. Interestingly, whilst Rosa wears rubber gloves adding to the medicalisation of the body and clearly delineating between the roles of carer and patient, Benigno does not. This is perhaps the first sign that he does not medicalise Alicia and that he is crossing over the patient/carer boundary. It is also important to note that throughout, even when Alicia has make up on with her hair done, she has tracheotomy tube sticking out of her neck helping her to breathe; a constant reminder of the fact that she is, despite Benigno's imagination, a very sick woman.

Almodóvar used elements of the **Stanislavsky method** when preparing his actors for the screen, and trained Javier and Rosa in nursing, spending time with coma patients in order to enhance the medicalised representation of Alicia's body. He said:

> Both Mariola and Javier did everything 'for real'. From the script, I emphasized that the actors should show their skill as nurses. Only in that way could one understand the total dependence of a body in a vegetative state.[5]

The Body and Religious Symbolism

In a particular bird's-eye view at the end of the opening hospital scene, Benigno and the nurse pull back the covers and lay over a dress with ties at the side. The shot dissolves to show the passage of time. Alicia doesn't move throughout the duration of these long takes making her appear somewhat like a corpse being dressed for their casket. The long white dress could equally be interpreted as making Alicia look like a virgin bride and has something of the air of fairy tale sleeping beauty about her. During the *Shrinking Lover*/rape scene Benigno tells Alicia he is going to rub her with rosemary alcohol. Throughout the film Benigno seems to be constantly rubbing products into Alicia's skin as if trying to preserve her. He even does this to Lydia, who is not his patient, rubbing Vaseline into her lips. Robert B. Pippin describes the dressing of Alicia as 'ritualistic' and 'religious'.[6] One could interpret that some of these shots echo biblical imagery of Jesus before the resurrection:

> Taking Jesus' body, the two of them wrapped it, with the spices, in strips of linen. This was in accordance with Jewish burial customs. (John 19:14)

She poured perfume on my body beforehand to prepare for my burial.[7] (Mark 14:8)

The idea of embalming puts Benigno in a feminine Mary Magdalene role and Alicia is literally his deity or goddess to be worshiped. Like Jesus, she will be resurrected as she awakens miraculously from her coma.

Lydia's room has more obvious religious symbolism in it, with a small shrine prepared by her sister with images of saints and a burning candle. The room becomes like a tomb. Unlike Alicia who is kept more alive by Benigno's passion for her, Marco says of Lydia '...her brain is turned off' making her symbolically dead.

Nature, the Landscape and the Body

Whilst Almodóvar's films are relentlessly urban, it is interesting to look at the role that nature and the landscape has within the film and how the body is often transfigured as a landscape. Most of Almodóvar's films including *Talk to Her* are set in Madrid; however, Almodóvar often features a return to the rural village in his narratives in films such as *The Flower of My Secret* and *What Have I Done to Deserve This?* This return to the countryside often represents a kind of redemption for characters. Although in *Talk to Her* there is no return to the village, Benigno ends his life in the countryside in the rural prison outside Segovia.

Several people, including C.D.C Reeve, have made the parallel with the final dance and the biblical metaphor for the Garden of Eden and viewing the ending in this way, one can view it also as the characters now being able to be part of nature and the landscape.[8] The stage design is a dense wall of vines, textured like a vertical landscape, complemented by the floral patterns of the women's dresses.

In *Talk to Her*, a direct parallel is made between the landscape of Spain and the human body. Whilst Marco and Lydia are seen driving through Spain's landscape, Alicia cannot travel or experience this landscape, trapped not only in a coma but also in her hospital room. It is her body, then, that becomes a landscape. The most explicit parallel is made during the *Shrinking Lover* sequence where Alfredo Is seen climbing over Amparo's body as if it were a landscape, her breasts resembling mountains which he struggles to climb (Fig. 5). This parallel is further heightened by a round mirror in the back of the scene that appears to suggest a moon.

Fig. 5

landscape, her breasts resembling mountains which he struggles to climb (Fig. 5). This parallel is further heightened by a round mirror in the back of the scene that appears to suggest a moon.

Additionally, the framing of Alicia's body and face create some unusual landscapes. Typically in cinema, as one might expect, people's faces are shot in portrait; however, as Alicia is lying down for much of the film, her face and body are often filmed like scenery in landscape. The effect is unusual, causing the spectator to want to tilt their head. In another shot the camera is placed on the bed behind her head in a shallow focus close up; an unusual angle to see anyone, even in real life. Her face appears morphed and distorted, her body behind it is fleshy and indistinct like the rolling hills of the Spanish agricultural landscape.

The parallel between nature and the body is made more explicit in the name of the hospital, El Bosque, meaning The Forest. One could also draw a comparison with fairy tales notably Snow White who, is trapped in a coma like state, preserved in a glass box just as Lydia is often filmed through the glass windows of the hospital room as if from the point of view of the forest. Interestingly, a correlation between bull fighting and fairy tales is made in *Blancanieves*, a Spanish film made in the style of a silent movie. It retells the story of Snow White but in Spain in 1910 following a young girl, Carmen, whose father is a famous bull fighter who runs away from her wicked step mother and joins a troupe of bull fighting dwarves.

Muñoz states, that in Almodóvar's earlier films 'the human body as one of the locales of negotiation, tension and trauma' and suggests that the body is acts as 'a sign of the social contradictions of a country involved in a process of profound cultural transition'[9]. This could be referring to some of the more obvious physical transformations of the body in films such as *All About My Mother*, which features transgender and transsexual characters. Muñoz suggests that this body narrative continues in *Talk to Her* with Alicia's awakening concluding the film 'with a renewed promise of reconstructing and rebuilding the nation'.[10] Alicia's body can be seen as a metaphor for Spain, culturally and expressively asleep under Franco and its symbolic reawakening after the death of Franco.

Dance

Dance is probably the most obvious motif alluding to the theme of **corporeality**; the nature of the physical body. The inclusion of dance also brings up issues of communication and the theme of the intimate stranger. Piña Bausch was a German dancer and choreographer whose choreographies feature at the beginning and end of *Talk to Her* and who features as a dancer in the first performance. Bausch's style, like Almodóvar's, can be described as postmodernist in that it broke down strict divisions of high and low art in her work, combining dance with other art forms such as theatre, cinema and opera. Similarly her work was often choreographed to different styles of music such as jazz, pop and world music.

Almodóvar's inclusion of Bausch's choreography can be read in several different ways, firstly as a celebration of European culture. Throughout Almodóvar's work he creates intertextual links and references to aspects of culture he enjoys, whether it be through theatre, in *All About My Mother*'s reference to Tennessee Williams' play *A Streetcar Named Desire*, or homage to the female lead punk genre in *Pepi, Luci, Bom*. Another interpretation could be that the film could be read as being about bodies and physicality and beginning and ending the film with explicit visual reference to the body and physical movement establishes and reasserts these themes. A third interpretation could be that the narrative of the whole film is somewhat like a dance with men and women dancing together; trying to connect then dancing alone before finally swapping dance partners (Marco and Alycia).

Writing for the London-based dance theatre Sadler's Wells brochure for Piña Bausch's choreography Nelken & Palermo Palermo, Almodóvar wrote:

> In *Todo sobre mi madre (All About My Mother)* there was a poster of Piña in Café Müller (it was hanging on a wall in Cecilia Roth's son's room). I didn't know then that that choreographic piece would be the prologue to my next film. At the time I only wanted to pay homage to the German choreographer. When I finished writing *Talk To Her* and looked at Piña's face again, with her eyes closed, and at how she was dressed in a flimsy slip, her arms and hands outstretched, surrounded by obstacles (wooden tables and chairs), I had no doubt that it was the image which best represented the limbo in which my story's protagonists lived. Two women in a coma who, despite their apparent passivity, provoke the same solace, the same tension, passion, jealousy, desire and disillusion in men as if they were upright, eyes wide open and talking a mile a minute.[11]

The penultimate dance taken from Bausch's choreography *Masurca Fogo* is set to kd lang's song 'Hain't it Funny'. The melancholy lyrics seem to fit with some of the themes and narrative of the film.

> We made love last night, wasn't good, wasn't bad
> Intimate strangers made me kinda sad, period
> Now when I woke up this morning, coffee wasn't on
> It slowly dawned on me that my baby is gone
> My baby's gone.[12]

The song and the dance itself seems to highlight the absence of Benigno and the loss felt by Marco in lyrics like 'my baby's gone'. The idea of intimate strangers also resonates throughout the film. Despina Kakoudaki states

> *Intimate Strangers* can indeed describe many relationships in this film and is an especially apt interpretation of the secretive and mysterious relationship between Benigno and Alicia. Intimate strangers may always

be what people remain to each other- our struggle for understanding [...] efforts to overcome or counteract our distance from each other.[13]

The idea of intimacy is explored throughout the film. The film questions how intimacy can be achieved – whether it is physically through touch in the way that Benigno touches Alicia; through shared common interest in the way that Benigno takes on Alicia's interests such as dance and old films; or for Marco and Lydia, the façade of intimacy that comes from declaring yourself to be a couple. The dance features a woman sighing into a microphone with a long cord. Like Alicia and Lydia she is horizontal. She is carried along by a series of men's hands, similar to the way in which, in early scenes within the film we see shots of Alicia being washed by four hands disembodied by the tight framing of the shot or the shot in which Lydia is carried from the bullring. In her movement across the stage she is touched by the men; however like Alicia, she seems oblivious to their attention, looking in the opposite direction.

The concept of strangers is very important to the scene and the film as a whole. The idea that men and women can be physically close whilst simultaneously strangers to each other is explored through the performance and physicality. The woman, dressed in a feminine red floral dress is carried by the men who all wear the same white shirt and black trousers. As they lift and let her fall, she never looks at them. Like Alicia, the female dancer's movements are aided by men whom she cannot acknowledge.

References

1.   Freeland, Cynthia in Eaton, A.W (2009) *Philosophers on Film: Talk to Her*. Oxon: Routledge. p. 81

2.   Almodóvar, Pedro. Press Pack www.sonyclassics.com/talktoher/talktoher.pdf. p. 19

3.   Freeland, p. 76

4.   Freeland, p. 76

5.   Almodóvar, Pedro. Press Pack. p. 20

6.   Pippin, Robert B. in Eaton, A.W (2009) *Philosophers on Film: Talk to Her*. Oxon: Routledge. p. 34

7.   The Bible: contemporary English version (2000). London: Harper Collins

8. Reeve, C.D.C. in Eaton, A.W (2009) *Philosophers on Film: Talk to Her*. Oxon: Routledge. p. 104

9. Muñoz, Ernesto Acevedo. (2007) *World Directors: Pedro Almodóvar*. London: British Film Institute Acevedo. p. 240

10. Muñoz, p. 241

11. Almodóvar, Pedro. www.sadlerswells.com/pina-bausch/pedro-Almodóvar-talks-about-pina-bauschs-influence-on-his-films/ (accessed 27/09/14)

12. kd lang (1997) *Hain't it Funny*. Warner Bros. Records Inc

13. Kakoudaki, Despina in Edt. Epps, Bradley and Kakoudaki, Despina. (2007) *All about Almodóvar: A Passion for Cinema*. Minneapolis: Minessota University Press

Messages and Values: Rape and Moral Ambiguity

On first screening of the film, the spectator is placed in an unusual and morally ambiguous position. We grow to feel sympathy for Benigno and see him as the protagonist of the film. As we never see the rape, we are spared from upsetting imagery and as Alicia is in a coma and thus unable to resist, we are protected from the violence and force that usually accompanies cinematic depictions of rape. Added to this is the challenging fact that Benigno feels that the sex was an act of mutually understood love rather than a carer taking advantage of a patient. Furthermore the film delivers the highly problematic message that rape is somehow beneficial for Alicia.

Dominique Russell explores the moral ambiguities of rape as 'a trauma that depends on interpretation and the possibility of multiple truths'.[1] It is true that Benigno rapes Alicia and was attracted to her inanimate body; yet it is equally true that Benigno felt he was in a relationship with Alicia and believed that she would one day wake up. It is true that Benigno violated Alicia's inanimate body but it is equally true that he means her no harm and is caring towards her. *Talk to Her*, as with other art films, asks the spectator to reflect and engage with their own attitudes and values, and controversially, to consider whether some types of rape are 'worse' than others.

Noël Carroll considers *Talk to Her* an 'unsettling film because of the way in which it splits apart the tidy, coordinated, negative set of verdicts that we typically issue when morally condemning an act [...] *Talk to Her* puts us in the unfamiliar position of feeling the pressure to vote for a mixed decision.'[2] The rational spectator will know that rape is bad, but the film forces us to question several aspects of the rape which are morally problematic such as; is the fact that she was raped whilst in a coma (and thus unable to remember it) a lesser crime than a rapist who violently assaults their conscious victim, who is all too aware?

In *Talk to Her* the rape is masked by Benigno's retelling of the silent film 'The Shrinking Lover'. This protects the viewer from viewing Benigno as a sexual abuser just as earlier, the framing of Marco killing the snake obscures obscures the act of killing. Similarly, during the second bullfight the editing cuts briefly away to mask the brief moment where Lydia is penetrated during the goring sequence. The light hearted nature of the

Silent Lover film, combined with the comic **hyper-reality** of the vagina into which the film's protagonist enters, distracts the viewer from the seriousness of what is happening/ is about to happen.

To make things even more morally complex, Alicia wakes up from her coma after having the baby. This could put the spectator in a rather tricky position where we interpret the rape as having been 'good' for Alicia. Benigno is coded as an unlikely hero who saves the damsel in distress. The more one watches *Talk to Her*, the more complex the relationship the viewer has with the rape and the more we begin to question our loyalty as a viewer to the film's protagonist Benigno. For example, on first viewing one might assume that Benigno innocently believes that the sex is consensual however on second watching one notices how, upon undoing Alicia's dress straps Benigno hesitates and shakes his head saying 'no, I'm all right' emphasising, perhaps, that he realises that what he is about to do is morally wrong. Equally, by falsifying the records of her periods he demonstrates he is aware that he has done something that others will find morally reprehensible, to say the least.

Russell goes on to talk about the function of rape in art films, which she states 'serves as metaphor, symbol, plot device, character transformation, catalyst or narrative resolution.'[3] The rape in *Talk to Her* can be considered as a metaphor or symbol for several things, notably the symbolic rape of Spain under the dictator Franco, or as a symbol for Benigno reaching a delayed adolescence. The rape acts as a catalyst both in terms of the plot, with Benigno's imprisonment and subsequent suicide and Alicia's reawakening, but also crucially in Begnino's physical changes and personality development. As a result of the rape, ironically Benigno seems to accrue the qualities one might associate with a rapist: frustration and forcefulness.

In the self- interview for the film Almodóvar reveals his inspirations for the rape and its moral complexity:

> In the old Yugoslavia, a young night-shift guard of a morgue felt an attraction for a young dead woman. The loneliness of death joined to the loneliness of the night was too much loneliness, so the young guard follows his desires and takes the young deceased girl. What happened afterwards is one of those miracles of human nature which I don't think the Pope would really like. As a reaction to the love act, the dead girl

comes back to life. The young girl had a cataleptic illness and her death was only apparent. (I was not the only one who took note of this event. In France, two years ago, they made a film about this). Even though the family of the resurrected woman were really grateful to the rapist, they were not able to prevent him from going to jail. They took packets with food and got him a lawyer. A curious dilemma, the law took him as a simple rapist, but for the girl's family, who lived the reality according to their feelings, the guard had brought their girl back to life.[4]

This influence highlights the real life moral complexities associated with the rape in *Talk to Her* and how people can be simultaneously considered both deviant criminal and saviour just as Benigno is both a devoted carer and a deluded rapist.

Philosophy: Ethics and Aesthetics

In 2009, six US philosophy professors published the book *Talk to Her: Philosophers on Film*. The aim of the series in which the book appears is to look at film through the lens of philosophy. Noëll Carroll states that

Philosophy 'in' film [...] involves the interpretation of various motion pictures in terms of the standing philosophical themes that can be shown to illustrate, adumbrate, or articulate.[5]

Two schools of philosophy relevant to *Talk to Her* are aesthetics – the study of beauty, ugliness and truth – and ethics – the study of right and wrong. In any discussion of the aesthetics of film, one must first understand the components that make up the moving image, i.e. cinematography, performance, *mise-en-scène*, editing and sound. Just as in the aesthetic study of painting one might find the brush strokes or colour palette attractive or unpleasant, the study of aesthetics in film centres around images and sound that are either visually or audibly appealing or repellent. The aesthetics of a film and how aesthetically pleasing its elements are is hard to singularly define as aesthetics are subjective and based upon people's opinions of what they consider pleasing.

The ethics of film centres on the moral messages expressed through the narrative and characters and how these are interpreted. *Talk to Her* arguably presents situations to the spectator such as the rape and subsequent awakening, which provoke intellectual queries and judgemental responses.

The interplay between ethics and aesthetics is important within *Talk to Her* through the way in which repellent and immoral acts such as rape are presented in an aesthetically pleasing way. A. W. Eaton in her essay *Almodóvar's Immoralism* rejects autonomism, the idea that ethics and aesthetics must be considered as two separate entities and instead explores 'immoralism' as she suggests that the film is 'ethically defective' in the way in which it represents rape and Benigno as a rapist.[6] She states that 'moral and artistic value do not exist in separate airtight compartments but, rather, can impinge upon each other[7]' and sums up by asserting that 'the film is good (artistically) precisely because it is bad (ethically)'. She cites the effect upon the spectator who feels an ethical dilemma throughout the film, 'torn between feelings of sympathy and antipathy, attraction and disgust, praise and blame'.[8]

Similarly, commenting upon how the aesthetic pleasures of the films' technical elements sugarcoat the darker themes of rape, voyeurism and obsession, Thomas Sotinel writes:

> The softness of Javier Aguirresarobe's (the cinematographer) images and the melancholy grace of Alberto Iglesias's score together make *Talk to Her* a film whose daring is hidden behind a gentle sweetness.[9]

Comas and Rape in Myth and Film

The idea that one can be simultaneously physically alive but unconscious/mentally dead holds a place within cinematic discourse from films in diverse genres such as *Kill Bill: Vol. 1* (2003; action), the obviously named *Coma* (1977; paranoid thriller) and *The Dead Zone* (1983; horror/thriller). Interestingly for *Talk to Her*, the coma is used frequently in the romance genre, as in *While You Were Sleeping* (1995), *The Vow* (2012) and *Just like Heaven* (2005) as if the idea of a coma (or the amnesia that sometimes follows) is somehow intrinsically romantic. What is common in all of these films is that the people in the comas do wake up (with either positive or negative consequences). Despite that fact that it is very unlikely for someone in Alicia's condition to wake up, cinema has made us believe that it is possible.

In *Talk to Her*, there is something of fantasy fairy tale in the way Alicia wakes from her coma with parallels to the Disney film versions of *Sleeping Beauty* (1959) and *Snow White and the Seven Dwarves* (1937).[10] Sleeping princesses, as if in a coma, are awoken by the kiss of a prince. The narrative of *Talk to Her* takes on a kind of mythic quality replacing the kiss with a rape. These stories, designed for children, completely gloss over the fact that the male protagonists are essentially **necrophiliacs**; attracted to women when in a corpse-like state. Furthermore they dwell little on the fact that the men kiss the princesses without their knowledge or consent. Our knowledge and acceptance of such narratives arguably allows the audience to find the rape less shocking and Alicia's awakening more believable and even romantic due to cinema's sometimes mythic treatment of comas. Muñoz states that the medium of cinema, in its ability to create fantasy, is problematic for the depiction of rape: 'Arguably the rape is diffused by Almodóvar's cinematic eye, made into something magical, mesmerising or "fantastic" like the movies themselves.'[11]

Both A.W Eaton and Adriana Novoa have compared the rape scene in *Talk to Her* to that of Tarantino's *Kill Bill: Vol. 1* where the rape of a coma patient is represented as monstrous and repellent with little doubt in the spectator's mind that this is an unethical event. The hospital ward in *Kill Bill* is dingy, with a grubby green and blue colour palette and low key lighting. The scene is shot in shot/reverse shot using high angle shots to look down at the vulnerable 'Bride' (Uma Thurman) and low angle shots to make her rapist look imposing and brutish. The abuse of patients is on an organised scale, with the male nurse acting as a pimp for the comatose 'Bride'. Unlike the clinical, hygienic care that Benigno offers in the brightly coloured warmly lit Forest Clinic, in *Kill Bill* rape is quite literally dirty. In contrast to Alicia who looks clean, pretty and made up, The Bride looks filthy and greasy. The male nurse hands a filthy tub of 'Vaselube' to a man dressed in a grubby shirt and trucker hat informing him that, 'The chick's cooch can get drier than a bucket of sand'. Unlike Alicia who is unable to react to her rape the Bride (recently awakened from her coma) bites the tongue out of her rapist's mouth and kills the male nurse by crushing his head in a steel door. In *Kill Bill* the rapist and the nurse are represented as necrophiliacs, whereas it is made clear that Benigno was first attracted to Alicia when she was conscious in the dance studio. What A.W. Eaton notes is that in *Kill Bill* Tarantino, unlike Almodóvar, 'offers the gruesome spectacle of a man clumsily mounting the hospital bed of a wan comatose woman [...he] neither sanitizes nor prettifies the event'.[12] In *Talk to Her* violin music, warm glowing lights and massage make the hospital seem more like a spa.

Whereas *Kill Bill* offers vulgar imagery, *Talk to Her* offers symbolism in the form of the lava lamp. As C.D.C. Reeve notes: 'The screen fills with a red phallic shape; it is a globule in the bedside lava lamp. Soon it thins out and divides, mimicking what we easily interpret as ejaculation and the fertilisation of an ovum.'[13] Note that the image of the lava lamp has been turned ninety degrees mirroring Alicia's horizontal body.

Almodóvar and Rape

Almodóvar could be said to be a specialist in creepy characters who, rather than being represented as sinister, are represented as sweet, charming or misunderstood as is arguably the case for Benigno and is apparent in films such as *Matador* and *Tie me Up! Tie me Down!* Rape is a common theme within Almodóvar's films and is presented in a variety of different ways but which are arguably all problematic and morally ambiguous. His very first feature film *Pepi, Luci, Bom* begins with a rape, this time, in another abuse of power, by a police officer. In *Kika*, rape is represented in a way that, like the large vagina in *Talk to Her*, is as funny as it is disturbing. In *Kika*, the title character (asleep like Alicia) awakes to find Paul Bazzo, an ex-porn star and escaped convict, raping her. The scene lasts an uncomfortably long time whilst Bazzo tries to break his record for number of orgasms in a row. During the scene Kika complains 'one thing is a rape.... This is something else, it's taking all day!'. The rape scene is, unbeknownst to Kika, being filmed and will later be broadcast on television. Unlike Alicia, who, we assume will never know she was raped, Kika is doubly humiliated by the rape; a comment on the harsh treatment of privacy by the mass media.

Whilst in *Talk to Her* the rape is of a sleeping woman by a virgin man, in *I'm So Excited!* the roles are reversed as the female Bruna, who like Benigno is also a virgin, becomes sexually aroused by drinking a Valencia cocktail laced with mescaline and has sex with a sleeping man who has been drugged with muscle relaxant. Like Alicia, the man is unable to give consent. Unlike *Talk to Her* where rape, in everyone's eyes but Benigno's is seen as abhorrent, in *I'm So Excited!* the rape is glossed over and laughed off.

Rape in Spanish Cinema

Rape is somewhat of a theme in Spanish Cinema as a whole and many reviews have drawn similarities between the Luis Buñuel Film *Viridiana* (1960) and *Talk to Her*. Buñuel can be seen as Almodóvar's predecessor in terms of being Spain's leading film-maker. Viridiana was made in 1960 in Spain but only actually released there in 1977, after the death of Franco due to the strict censorship laws in place at the time.

Viridiana tells the story of a young woman, soon to be a nun, who goes to stay with her benefactor uncle Don Jaime before taking her vows. Like many of Almodóvar's films, such as *All About My Mother* and *Bad Education* that include transvestites, it is hinted that Don Jaime might also be a cross-dresser as he tries on his dead wife's shoe and holds her corset up to himself. Like the Café Müller dance at the beginning of the film where dancers walk like somnambulists, Viridiana sleep walks in her night gown through Don Jaime's room. Transfixed by how similar Viridiana looks to his dead wife, Don Jaime dresses her up in his dead wife's wedding dress and drugs her (Fig. 1). When she wakes up the next morning Don Jaime tells her that he has raped her so that she can no longer be a nun. Viridiana is repulsed, but he later retracts this, stating that he didn't rape her but said so in order to keep her from leaving. Viridiana and the spectator are left confused and unsure about what really happened. There are several similarities with *Talk to Her*, firstly that the rapist (or would-be rapist) is, like Benigno, represented as benign. He saves a wasp who is drowning in water, quite literally playing on the phrase 'he couldn't hurt a fly'. Like Benigno, Don Jaime expresses that he is lonely and rarely goes outside. Similarly Don Jaime could be accused of being attracted to passive women as he places the drugged Viridiana into a corpse-like pose with her arms crossed over her chest. Like Benigno, Don Jaime also commits suicide but, unlike Benigno, Don Jaime feels remorse for what he has done.

Fig. 1

Talk to Her can thus be seen to continue in the tradition of European, Spanish and art house cinema as presenting rape as something ambiguous and open to multiple interpretations and representing rapists as lonely, caring but deeply flawed men.

'The Shrinking Lover' – Analysis

'The Shrinking Lover' film sequence is arguably the most pivotal in the whole film as it, and the rape that it masks, is the turning point within the narrative. The scene is filmed in black and white in a smaller square shaped frame to emulate the standard 1.33:1 aspect ratio used by most films during the silent era. The film is silent and accompanied by an orchestral and strings-based soundtrack. Intertitles appear revealing the story and Benigno's voiceover can be heard at times. In the **press pack** Almodóvar writes about his aims for accuracy in the filming:

> In order to prepare myself for the language of silent cinema, I saw my favourite silent films again, Griffith, F. Lang, Murnau, T. Browning... Sunrise was essential. I wanted to be true to the narrative and form of the time. I found it more attractive to struggle for accuracy than to break the rules. Except for some inevitable license, all the shots were done with a tripod. I didn't use a single travelling shot, in the composition of a shot the upper part of the frame is usually empty, the actors walk into frame, the props are authentic, from the mid-20s...[15]

The scene begins in a hyper real science lab. In another subversion of traditional gender stereotypes the 'mad scientist' is a woman, Amparo. Her boyfriend Alfredo seems unscientific and stands behind her smoking. Amparo accuses him of being selfish and only thinking of himself. Music is used in the silent film to help communicate emotions and feelings that one cannot express through dialogue. Played on strings, the music opens jauntily as Amparo and Alfredo argue flirtatiously. Whilst the images dissolve between elaborate science equipment, the music becomes discordant, establishing an uneasy atmosphere. The music builds to a crescendo signalling excitement as Amparo discovers her formula.

Almodóvar says that 'The Shrinking Lover' was inspired by two films:

> When I saw *Diabolical Dolls* or *The [Incredible] Shrinking Man* I always dreamt of making a film with a tiny man where the legs of furniture [...] were the main *mise-en-scène*.[16]

Diabolical Dolls (I am assuming he is referring to the 1936 film *The Devil Doll*, 'Diablo' meaning 'Devil' in Spanish), *The Incredible Shrinking Man* (1957) and Almodóvar's own 'Shrinking Lover' are theatrical and technical in the way that they are filmed. Enormous man-sized props like pens and letters were required as were large sets such as the enormous vagina. For a director who carefully plans his *mise-en-scène* this opportunity must have represented great deal of fun but also challenge. For potentially the first time in his career Almodóvar had to consider visual effects in depth, using models, green screen and super imposition.

In *The Devil Doll* there is a female mad scientist Malita on whom Almodóvar surely modelled Amparo, albeit as a younger more attractive version, with the same dark curly hair. It is likely that Amparo's over-the-top lab, all beakers and funnels which slowly dissolve into each other, are inspired by the fantastical *mise-en-scène* of Malita's lab (Fig. 2). Malita plans to continue the work of her late husband who has created a formula to shrink the human population down to a sixth of their size in order to make the world's resources last longer. Similarly to Almodóvar's films, in *The Devil Doll* there is also a fluid approach to gender with the film's central male protagonist Paul Lavond dressing as a woman to evade capture. Lavond uses the small people similarly to *Talk to Her*, but in a gender reversal, in one scene a female small person climbs up onto a bed and crawls over a sleeping figure of a man. She maims him (under

Fig. 2

Lavond's telepathic instruction) rendering the man paralysed. The line in *The Devil Doll*, 'A brilliant mind imprisoned in a useless body', seems also to sums up Alicia and Lydia's situation.

The performances of the two actors in 'The Silent Lover' are melodramatic; Amparo pushes Alfredo's face and jumps maniacally when she discovers the formula. In silent cinema, without the benefit of dialogue, performances had to be more theatrical with an exaggeration of facial expression and gesture in order to communicate. As a result, to modern audiences, performances seem campy and melodramatic. Silent cinema performers often emerged from the cabaret and theatre tradition and hence employed on film the same techniques as one would use to perform to large crowds – a style which Almodóvar was clearly trying to emulate. Almodóvar describes the performances of his two central actors:

> ...the acting is strictly expressionist, with a lot of care taken to avoid the risks of overacting. I was lucky that both Paz Vega and Fele Martínez could place themselves effortlessly in that situation which is so close to parody without ever succumbing to it. Their performances, naïf, tragic-comic and accurately expressionist, are due solely to their intuition and talent.[17]

Like movie stars of the silent era, the two actors male wear pale makeup with heavy eyeliner. This was done to counteract the harsh lighting and monochrome black and white film footage which would appear to flatten

Fig. 3

facial features. The effect on Alfredo makes him look arguably less masculine; combined with his chubbiness and small bow tie he looks comedic and effeminate (Fig. 3).

The strings keep a steady rhythm as Alfredo drinks the potion, building anticipation and a sense of urgency to what is otherwise an undramatic moment. Alfredo belches visibly in Amparo's face ruffling her hair; a moment of slapstick toilet humour adding to the overall light-hearted feel of the short film. The formula (and seemingly the belch!) act as an aphrodisiac and the pair kiss frantically. As Alfredo begins to shrink, the volume of the music increases as does the tempo, mirroring his dramatic jerking as the potion begins to take effect. The shot dissolves into another kiss. This time Alfredo is visibly smaller and Amparo is crying.

Alfredo is a paradox. On the one hand he has become more masculine, he has lost some of his puppy fat and is more sexually voracious; however, on the other hand he has visibly shrunk and is therefore emasculated. He continues to shrink and is shown in a mid-shot on an oversized table writing his leaving letter with an enormous pen. The next inter title says: 'To stop Amparo's suffering Alfredo left.' It is unclear exactly what is meant by this, but perhaps it implies that it is suffering for a woman to be with an emasculated man.

The next shot denotes Alfredo leaving the building; the music takes on a sadder tone with slow, high-pitched violin melodies. The proportions in this shot are disorientating. The building and door behind Alfredo are large but not unfeasibly so and yet Alfredo is carrying two very oversized suitcases which appear so heavy that he loses balance and stumbles slightly; again, the shot has the air of slapstick about it in the style of silent actors such as Buster Keaton, Charlie Chaplin or Laurel and Hardy. His mother is shot in a low angle shot and is represented as a formidable figure. She breathes heavily as if seething with rage as Amparo walks away with Alfredo, another example of a dysfunctional relationship within *Talk to Her*'s repertoire of broken families and overbearing mothers.

The couple check in to the Hotel Youkali. 'Youkali' was a Tango written by the German composer Kurt Weill, the lyrics of which speak of Youkali as being a mythical island of pleasure, desire and happiness. Considering it within this context, for Alfredo, Amparo's body is like Youkali; it is an island for his pleasure. At the end of the song the lyrics say that Youkali doesn't exist and it's just a dream, perhaps emphasising the element of fantasy about the film that Benigno fails to understand.

On the bed, Amparo and Alfredo have a conversation, but as spectators we have no idea what they are saying; another moment where communication between the genders is difficult. As Amparo goes to sleep, Alfredo mimics her, holding his hands to his tilted head. He is out of focus and Amparo appears gigantic behind him. Despite the fact that the films focus is on men, women are quite literally a larger more imposing force even when passive. As Peter Bradshaw, in his review of *Talk to Her* for The Guardian, notes, there is something of *Gulliver's Travels* about the scene, in Gulliver's visit to the mythical land of Brobdingnag where all of the people are giants and Gulliver is immensely small by comparison.[18]

Amparo falls asleep quickly, perhaps too quickly, as if drugged. Alfredo turns round with a determined look upon his face and wastes no time at all in pulling the covers from Amparo's naked, slumbering body just as, in the hospital, Benigno is pulling back Alicia's blanket and clothing. There is a momentary bird's-eye view shot of Amparo similar to the way Alicia's body is shot (Fig. 4). This is the first instance where a direct parallel can be brought between the two. Alfredo begins to tug at the lace sheet, pulling like a trawler man might pull in a net or adjust a ships rigging. The shot cuts to Amparo's pert breast revealed just as moments before we saw Alicia's breasts revealed. The shot cuts to an extreme close up of Amparo's eye rolling, perhaps in sleep or in implied pleasure. The slow

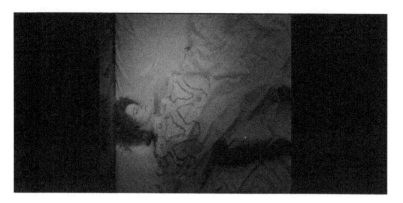

Fig. 4

string music increases in volume and pitch before Alfredo climbs upon her body and rolls around on her breasts as if he were in a large bouncy castle. He dives onto her left breast and then, like a dancer doing an arabesque, he sticks his leg out in apparent pleasure. Unlike the chubby man-child at the beginning of the film, this new Alfredo is nimble and boyish. Alfredo's shrinking seems to have awakened his sexuality just as watching the *Silent Lover* film seems to have awakened Benigno's sexuality. In an eye-line match sequence, Alfredo notices Amparo's pubic mound and is taken aback by it. In a long shot he walks across Amparo's body as if it were a landscape the mirror behind him resembles a moon, her legs and breasts are like hills. Alfredo clambers down before finding her vagina (for more on the body as a landscape see the chapter on Physicality and the Body).

The vagina is clearly fake with little attempt to make it look realistic. The hair looks dense and plasticky and as Alfredo enters it, the sides of the vagina pucker as if Amparo is inflatable or made of foam. Amparo's vagina is closer to that of a sex doll than to living flesh. Considering this in the context of Alicia, Benigno's rape seems even more perverse when sex with a comatose body is likened to sex with a sex doll.

As Alfredo reaches his arm into Amparo's vagina, with a clearly aroused expression on his face, the camera cuts to Amparo who is sleeping and appears not to realise what is happening; dwelling on the point that Alfredo has not received her consent. Alfredo looks at his arm, moist

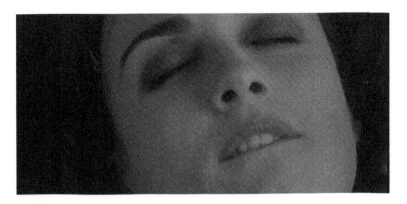

Fig. 5

from Amparo's vagina, and seems to almost go cross-eyed with arousal. He takes his top off and dives into her vagina head first. The scene again cuts to Amparo's indifferent face; like Alicia she is unaware of her penetration. Alfredo emerges closed-eyed and breathing heavily. He removes his underwear and dives in again, this time with his full body. The scene cuts again to Amparo's face. This time her expression is far from indifferent; she appears to be approaching orgasm, making an expression as if groaning with pleasure and then biting her lip (Fig. 5). The image is accompanied by a crescendo in the music quite literally signalling a climax. Like Alicia, Amparo has been raped, but, unlike Alicia who cannot experience anything, Amparo appears to have found the experience pleasurable which is a controversial and risky statement for any filmic depiction of rape to present. As if to highlight Alicia's inability to experience any pleasure from the encounter the silent film cuts from Amparo's face abruptly to Alicia's impassive face (Fig. 6); the music continues in a sound bridge further linking the two together.

Just as Almodóvar puts the spectator into an uncomfortable position in which we feel sympathy for a rapist in the case of Benigno, so too this scene, on initial watching, appears somewhat innocent and not like rape. Whilst Alicia and Benigno are not in reality a couple, Alfredo and Amparo are. Rape by definition is sexual penetration without consent. Alfredo does not have Amparo's consent to penetrate her. Just because Amparo and Alfredo are a couple does not mean it is not rape but, on a first viewing, it is quite possible to overlook this and enjoy in the faux silent cinema

Fig. 6

homage. But while Alfredo is unable to rape Amparo with his penis, as C.D.C. Reeve notes Alfredo shrinks to 'roughly the size of an erect penis'.[19] His whole body is a symbolic phallus and he quite rapes her with his entire being; an ultimate rape.

'The Shrinking Lover' ends with Benigno saying the line 'And Alfredo... stays inside her... forever'. As Almodóvar says, the story receives a narrative resolution in more ways than one 'an end [to] a cycle, finish back [to] where he started';[20] i.e. Alfredo emerged from a womb at birth and has now returned to it. If the film acts as a metaphor for Benigno's rape of Alicia, the fact that Benigno ejaculates in her creating a son could be seen as a metaphor for staying within her. The baby dies, just as we assume Alfredo will.

References

1. Russell, Dominique. (2010) *Rape in Art Cinema*. London: The Continuum International Publishing Group

2. Carroll, Noël in Edt. Eaton, A.W. (2009) *Philosophers on Film: Talk to Her*. Oxon: Routledge. p. 8

3. Russell, ibid.

4. Almodóvar, Pedro. Self-Interview www.sonyclassics.com/talktoher/flashwebsite/core/hasFlash.html (Accessed 29/09/14)

5. Carroll, p. 2

6. Eaton, AW. (2009) *Philosophers on Film: Talk to Her.* Oxon: Routledge. p. 20

7. Eaton, p. 21

8. Eaton, p. 22

9. Sotinel, Thomas. (2010) *Masters of Cinema: Pedro Almodóvar.* Paris: Cahiers Du Cinema Sarl. p. 79

10. Note that the original Brothers Grimm fairy tales are slightly different

11. Muñoz, Ernesto Acevedo. (2007) *World Directors: Pedro Almodóvar.* London: British Film Institute Acevedo. p. 261

12. Eaton, p. 16

13. Reeve, C.D.C in Edt. Eaton, A.W. (2009) *Philosophers on Film: Talk to Her.* Oxon: Routledge. p. 99

14. Almodóvar, Pedro. Self-Interview

15. Almodóvar, Pedro. Self-Interview

16. Almodóvar, Pedro. Self-Interview

17. Bradshaw, Peter. (Friday 23rd August 2002) *Talk to Her* www.theguardian.com/film/2002/aug/23/1 (accessed 19/09/14)

18. Reeve, p. 98

19. Edt. Strauss, Frederic. (2006) *Almodóvar on Almodóvar.* London: Faber and Faber. p. 221

Psychoanalysis

Film's relationship with psychoanalysis is as old as the medium itself. Eighteen ninety-five, the year of the first film screening, was also the year Sigmund Freud published the first book to identify psychoanalysis as a form of treatment. In a very basic sense psychoanalysis is the study of the struggle between the conscious and unconscious mind and the impact of childhood sexuality on adult life. As Vicky Lebeau suggests:

Very quickly cinema becomes a way of talking about, of picturing the mind for psycho analysis – just as the mind becomes one way to consider the mechanism and fascination of cinema.[1]

Cinema, in a way that no other art form can do successfully, allows us to experience memory and dream in a visual way through flashbacks, dream sequences, fantasy sequences and voiceovers, thus giving us an insight into the internal world or psychology of the character.

Part of Freud's theories of psychoanalysis was that of dream analysis. Lebeau compares watching a film to be like experiencing a dream and thus, when we analyse and interpret characters, we are to a certain extent as a spectator conducting a Freudian analysis of the character. She says:

Like the psychoanalyst, the spectator of cinema can become an astute interpreter, a reader of public dreams.[2]

During the 1970s psychoanalytic film theory became a popular mode for analysing film. For the purposes of studying *Talk to Her*, three aspects of psychoanalytic film theory can be interesting; the unconscious of the film-maker, the unconscious of the character and the film interacting with the unconscious of the audience.

Early Psychoanalytic Film Theory invited the spectator to decode the unconscious of the film-maker, seeing film as a projection or expression of the film-maker's unconscious. Analysing *Talk to Her* in this way could see the film as a manifestation of Almodóvar's unconscious. For Almodóvar this approach could be fruitful, as several people including Suzie McKenzie have claimed that *Talk to Her* and his subsequent film *Bad Education* are somewhat autobiographical.[3] For example, male bonding was probably an important theme in Almodóvar's childhood growing up as he did in an all male environment in a monastery training to be a priest. The theme of abuse of power and seemingly benevolent people being sexually perverse could come from his experience of seeing the sexual abuse carried out by members of the priesthood during his time there. One could also speculate that as an unmarried man in his fifties, Almodóvar may have himself experienced loneliness in his life like Marco and Benigno. Added to this, Almodóvar's *mise-en-scène* includes a host of influences and elements from aspects of culture he has enjoyed; thus through the film we get hints of Almodóvar's taste and personality (see chapter on *mise-en-scène* for more) giving us hints and insights into his psyche.

The second branch of psychoanalytic film theory focuses on characters and the audience's challenge and desire to analyse their unconscious motivations. Whilst this approach has been criticised, as arguably characters, by their very nature, are not real and thus *have no unconscious*, it can prove fruitful in an analysis of *Talk to Her* particularly through the explicit references to psychiatry and Benigno's past. From a film director who normally presents females as his central protagonists, *Talk to Her* makes it hard for the spectator to engage in an analysis of the unconscious mind of its female protagonists who are non-communicative for much of the film.

The third branch of psychoanalytic film theory is audience-centred, which sees characters' behaviours as being interpreted as explorations of the spectator's own unconscious. Thus when we see characters on screen, their actions help to define, reassert or re-evaluate our own sense of self. This approach is similarly interesting to consider due to the interesting position in which it places the spectator in relation to Benigno and the rape and forces us to ask difficult questions (see chapter Rape and Moral Ambiguity).

Analysing Benigno

The inclusion of psychoanalysis as a theme is made explicit through Benigno's visit to Alicia's father Dr Roncero, a psychologist. However, even if this had not been included arguably the audience would have still identified the theme within the film. Almodóvar says of the film:

It is also a film about madness, about a type of madness so close to tenderness and common sense that it does not diverge from normality.[4]

During this scene Benigno is asked about his sexual experiences. He says he has had none, and instead describes how he lacked a father during his upbringing and intimately cared for his mother who was not ill but lazy. Naturally, due to Benigno's unusual descriptions of his childhood, his blind unrequited love for Alicia and his inability to understand why others would find his 'relationship' strange, the spectator analyses Benigno in much the same way a psychologist might analyse a patient.

Sigmund Freud was particularly interested in how infant sexuality and relationships with parents influenced a person's psychology. In a simplified form Freud's Oedipus complex can be broken down into four steps.

1. As a small boy, the child is attached emotionally to his mother and does not wish to share her.

2. The child is jealous of the father.

3. The child fears castration anxiety (that the father will punish him by cutting of his penis).

4. The boy overcomes his fear by repressing his desire for his mother and begins to forge his identity as a male.[5]

It is important to remember that Freud's Oedipus complex is a theory and that it has been disputed by those who have studied atypical families such as single mothers, homosexual parents or cultures where mothers and fathers take on different roles to that of typical western families. This said, the Oedipus complex is a useful tool in attempting to psychoanalyse Benigno. Dr Roncero refers to Benigno's upbringing as 'special', and within the context of Freud's Oedipus complex it appears just that. It is significant that Benigno's father left the family at the age of four, around the age that, according to the Oedipus complex, a child begins to feel jealousy of the father. Benigno has arguably not progressed from the first stage and has thus not developed his sexuality and identity as a male. He says casually that he scrubbed his mother 'front and back'. Clearly his attachment to his mother, whilst not necessarily itself sexual, was unhealthy in terms of his own sexual development.

One can also consider social learning theory and apply it to Benigno's unusual upbringing as a way of understanding him. Social learning theory, with regard to gender, is the idea that as children, boys and girls act in a certain way according to their gender because they are expected to act in a certain way by their parents/ other adults. Thus, they learn to behave in a gendered way accordingly. If we consider Benigno's upbringing, far from his mother expecting him to take on 'the man of the house' role as is often the case in films with absent fathers, Benigno has been expected to take on a caring role by his mother; a typically feminine attribute. Not only was his childhood and adolescence spent almost entirely with women, but equally he works in a female centred environment. If we take social learning theory in its most literal sense, Benigno has not been expected to, nor has he learnt how to, be a man. Viewing the film in this way, one can say that the influence of Marco has a profound effect on Benigno's gender development.

Furthermore, it seems odd that having been with Alicia for four years, it is only after meeting and becoming friends with a masculine male (Marco) that he rapes Alicia (we are assuming of course that this is the first time he has done it). The implication here would be that from Marco he has learnt how to 'be a man' and, therefore, his previous childlike crush on Alicia has evolved into 'mature' sexual desire. This could also be interpreted according to Gender-Schema Theory – the idea that children observe and then take on traits of the gender they identify with. Up until this point, Benigno has had few men in his life whose traits he can observe. This may also explain why some argue that Benigno and Marco grow in similarity particularly during the later prison scenes, perhaps because Benigno is mimicking some of Marco's masculine traits.

The formation of personality, likes, and dislikes, develops at its peak during adolescence. However, even into adulthood Benigno's personality can be thought of as a blank template. During the conversation with Alicia he says, 'May I walk you there, I've got nothing to do.' Alicia asks him what he does when he goes out to which Benigno replies 'I don't go out.' Just as Benigno becomes imprisoned later in the film, his life with his mother can be thought of as an imprisonment. While his mother is alive we only see Benigno in the flat or at work. It is only after his mother has died that he ventures out. Benigno only gains a personality through taking on Alicia's hobbies and interests. His conversation with Alicia lasts for minutes but during that time he gains the information that will shape his character for the next four years. He watches dance at the theatre, he visits the Cinémathèque to watch silent movies and later, reads Marco's travel guides in order to indulge his/ Alicia's interests in dance, cinema and travel (even though it's possible that the farthest Benigno may have travelled in his life is from Madrid to Segovia when he is taken to prison). Having been essentially trapped in his house for most of his upbringing, Benigno, like a prisoner, has learned about life from reading books and magazines. He decorates his flat from an image seen in an advert and orders the whole lot rather than developing his own tastes and sense of self from social and cultural experiences (Fig. 1).

Fig. 1

As mentioned, part of Freud's method of psychoanalysis was dream analysis. Initially this seems unimportant to the film. There are no dream sequences as such, however George M. Wilson suggests that 'The Shrinking Lover' sequence could be a dream-like manifestation of Benigno's psyche.

> Has Benigno seen such a movie? Certainly, we know he has seen a poster for a movie with that title, but even the most Expressionist cinema of the 1920s did not really produce anything so peculiar in the manner of this film. Or are we seeing Benigno's private fantasy of a movie he has seen – a private screening, so to speak, of his dominant psychological preoccupations?[6]

Indeed, whereas we see Benigno in the audience while he recounts his version of the Café Müller dance performance to Alicia, we never see him actually *in* the cinema watching the film. If the film is a manifestation of Benigno's desires then it certainly fits with Almodóvar's own experience of telling films, i.e. making up one's own stories based loosely on film plots:

> I remember when I was little I would tell films to my sisters, films that we had seen together. I'd get carried away by the memory and while I was trying to remember I'd reinvent them. Really I was making my own adaptation, and my sisters preferred my inaccurate, delirious versions to the original film.[7]

This idea of misremembering and adapting memories is central to psychoanalysis and to the analysis of Benigno and Marco who both recount stories of the past in the film. What Benigno may have done, is taken a rather tamer and less sexually charged silent film and projected his own sexual desires onto the stories resolution. When he is recounting the tale of 'The Shrinking Lover', he compares Alfredo, the central character, to himself, describing him as 'a bit overweight like me but a nice guy', as if putting himself in the story. The word 'nice' here is important as it confirms Benigno's delusions about himself. He still considers himself to be a nice guy even though he is about to rape Alicia. The story ends with what could be said to be an Oedipal crisis; a return to the womb and to the symbolic mother.

Benigno as a Psychopath

During the prison sequence, Benigno tells Marco that his lawyer has referred to him as a psychopath. The term 'psychopath' is commonly associated with antisocial behaviour, a lack of remorse, the inability to love, arrogance and dangerous, violent, callous behaviour.[8] The Chambers dictionary defines psychopathy to be:

> A personality disorder characterized by an inability to from close relationships, the rejection of authority, and little or no remorse for what they have done.[9]

Certainly some of these words seem to fit Benigno. He has little remorse for what he has done because he can't understand why it was wrong; he seems to place the blame on the system (authority) for not understanding what he and Alicia had together. However, other aspects of the psychopath definition don't fit. While he doesn't have many friends, he is not antisocial and is jovial with the nurses, some of whom, such as Rosa, even stand up for him. He definitely has the ability to love even if the object of his love is severely misguided and he has proven, through his friendship with Marco, that he has the ability to form close relationships. While this instance of rape might be deemed similar to necrophilia, the film does not make Benigno out to be a necrophiliac; we do not get the sense that he is attracted to Alicia just *because* she is inanimate but *in spite of* the fact she is inanimate. Benigno first seems to fall in love with Alicia whilst she is being active, as he views her in the dance studio.

Arrogance is a word not easy to attach to Benigno who, for parts of the film, is self-deprecating, asserting that he is chubby and lonely. Is Benigno dangerous? Possibly to Alicia but not in a wider sense. His name Benigno meaning benign and his insistence that he is 'harmless' suggest at least that he doesn't consider himself to be dangerous. Is Benigno violent? The fact that we are spared from witnessing any violence in the film would suggest that at least we are not meant to view him in this way. Almodóvar says of Benigno: 'Benigno is insane, but he has a good heart. He's a gentle psychopath.'[10]

Obsession

Both Marco and Benigno have obsessive personalities. Marco has taken ten years to get over his previous love interest Angela, and Benigno has been obsessed with Alicia we assume for at least four and a half years (and possibly much longer).

Benigno has also demonstrated stalker tendencies. J. Reid Meloy, a forensic psychologist, outlines several characteristics of real stalkers that one can associate with Benigno. First, that with most stalkers there is a 'history of failed intimate relationships' and furthermore, that stalking is often a 'maladaptive response to social incompetence, social isolation and loneliness.'[11] With this in mind, we can perhaps understand Benigno's stalking as a response to the fact that he has never experienced or witnessed a normal romantic relationship and thus believes that his behaviour towards Alicia before her accident to be romantic and normal. Certainly, the flashback scene where he recounts the story of how he and Alicia met is presented somewhat like a romantic film, in an intimate two shot with Alicia smiling and keen to chat. Our reaction as a spectator is also influenced by Marco's lack of outrage in his reaction to Benigno's tale, allowing us to accept Benigno's dreamy storytelling. The cinematography also helps to deceive the audience into imagining that this is a love story through the framing of Alicia. Often in classic Hollywood cinema before a flashback, the camera will zoom in on the person's face who is having the flashback; a visual signifier that we are about to enter the internal world of the character either through memory, dream or imagination. However, rather than it being Benigno's face we zoom into, it is Alicia's; implying that it is *her* memory (Fig. 2). As much as Benigno might like to think this is a happy memory shared with Alicia, this is very unlikely to be true, and thus reasserts how delusional he is.

Fig. 2

During a scene where the nurses gossip about Benigno and Marco the following conversation takes place:

NURSE 2: He isn't a faggot too, is he?

NURSE 1: No way, are you nuts?

ROSA: Are you insinuating that Benigno is a faggot?

NURSE 2: *I'm* not, its vox populi, honey.

ROSA: You're very wrong.

NURSE 2: Dr Vega confirmed it for me.

The conversation is interesting as it implies that Rosa, who storms off, might herself have feelings for Benigno. This is potentially disturbing: if we regard Benigno as a bumbling, lonely, loser with no hope of getting a date with a conscious woman then one might, perhaps, sympathise with his obsession for Alicia. However, if Benigno is considered desirable by a walking, talking co-worker, one might interpret his actions towards Alicia as being much more sinister.

Benigno says that Alicia's dance studio is opposite his house but this is not *strictly* true; it is on an angle, a fair distance from Benigno's window. The beginning of the flashback involves an eye-line match sequence whereby Benigno stands at the window looking out across at the dance studio. The first of Benigno's point-of-view shots is realistic and in long shot (Fig. 3). As a consequence, Alicia is a small figure who is hard to pick out from the crowd. To have singled her out at this distance above all the other dancers seems illogical, particularly as he has never seen her face to face. The shot cuts back to Benigno's face looking earnestly and then cuts again to a medium close up of Alicia (Figs 4 & 5). This shot would be impossible for Benigno to see, not least because there are two panes of glass separating them. During this whole sequence Alicia's gaze is firmly looking forward; she never turns her head in Benigno's direction to suggest that there is a connection between them.

Fig. 3

Figs 4 & 5

Like a hunter, Benigno seems to have sniper sharp vision. This is demonstrated by his noticing of Alicia's wallet falling on the floor from a reasonable distance and from being able to see which button Alicia presses on the keypad of her building from across the street. We never see him with binoculars – this would make his stalker credentials explicit – but through the way some sequences are shot one can make one of two assumptions. Firstly we could assume that he is using binoculars but the spectator is spared from the negative connotations of considering Benigno as a stalker or pervert. Secondly, we could conceive that after months/ years of observing he has honed his skills in noticing minute details about Alicia.

In 1993 Zona and colleagues defined stalkers into three categories: the 'simple obsessional' where the victim of stalking is often an ex-lover and therefore the stalking is motivated by control; 'love obsessional stalkers' who are in love with their victims but do not believe that their victims are in love with them; and 'erotomanic stalkers' who don't know their victims, who are often celebrities, and think that their victims are in love with them[12]. Interestingly Benigno seems to have developed from a 'love obsessional' stalker to an 'erotomanic stalker' through the act of caring – we assume, that in his relationship with his mother, love was associated with caring, so it would make sense that Benigno believes the act of taking care of Alicia has made her fall in love with him. Thus, in his mind, his love is no longer unrequited.

Watching and Voyeurism

During the 1970s film theorists like Laura Mulvey used psychoanalytic film analysis to understand how gender bias and stereotypes are formed through the psychology of looking, notably through voyeurism and **scopophilia** which both are explored throughout *Talk to Her*. The very opening shot invites the spectator to watch as red curtains rise up at the theatre. We, like Benigno and Marco, are positioned in the theatre audience watching most of the action in long shot as we are again at the end of the film. From then on, there are many instances of characters watching and particularly watching women. Marco first notices Lydia when watching her on TV; later he watches her at the bull fight and then at the hospital. Similarly, Marco watches Alicia, first through the door at the hospital, later at the dance studio and again at the theatre. Additionally, Benigno first watches Alicia when looking out of his window at the dance studio just as later he watches her as she sleeps.

Almodóvar has often been likened to Hitchcock in his filmic style. Hitchcock's film *Rear Window* (1954) may, in its themes of voyeurism, have inspired some of the shots in *Talk to Her*. In *Rear Window* L.B. Jefferies (James Stewart), like Benigno, is stuck in his house. Unlike Benigno who is kept there by a need to care for his mother, thus emotionally disabled, Jefferies has been physically disabled with his leg in a cast. Bored and frustrated, he spends his days looking out the window at his neighbours. The difference, however, is that in *Rear Window* the voyeuristic gaze is not restricted to one person as it is for Benigno, as L.B. Jefferies watches all of his neighbours. While Jefferies develops similar obsessive qualities to Benigno, he is capable of having a relationship with a real woman; the much younger Lisa, played by Grace Kelly.

Benigno could also be likened somewhat to another of Hitchcock's voyeuristic characters; that of Norman Bates from the film *Psycho* (1960). Like Benigno, Norman Bates lives alone with his mother and, like Benigno, Norman watches a woman; his motel guest Marion. Whereas Benigno watches Alicia from afar, Norman watches Marion through a small hole in the bathroom wall. He is physically much closer to and hidden from Marion making his voyeurism appear much more sinister. While Norman Bates can be thought of as a true psychopath (with murderous tendencies and a split personality disorder) Benigno is represented as much more innocent despite his delusions. Although both Bates and L.B. Jefferies spy on women in their underwear, it is important from a spectator empathy viewpoint that Benigno is not peering into Alicia's bedroom from his window but instead looking through the dance studio window. Arguably Benigno falls in love with Alicia's body but in a way that is romanticised. Alicia's body as a dancer is represented as a work of art to be admired. If Benigno was watching Alicia get dressed in her bedroom, her body would be eroticised and the spectator would be unable to see Benigno as anything more than a pervert or peeping tom. It is interesting to note that in *Talk to Her*, as in Hitchcock and indeed most cinema, voyeurism is a gendered activity with men possessing the gaze and women often unknowingly looked at.

The concept of voyeurism within film theory and criticism has been approached through several avenues. The first is through psychoanalytic film theory and the second is through feminist film criticism, considering voyeurism for the most part as gendered and the cinema positioning the viewer to look from a male point of view.

Gendered Spectatorship

Talk to Her is an interesting film to study in relation to Laura Mulvey's concept of the male gaze. In her paper 'Visual Pleasure in Narrative Cinema' (1975), Mulvey outlined her theory, the basic concept of the male gaze being that viewing at the cinema is a gendered activity and as spectators (whether male or female) we are guided to view women from a male perspective and objectify them. She says:

> In a world ordered by sexual imbalance, pleasure in looking has been split between active/male and passive/female. [...] In their traditional exhibitionist role women are simultaneously looked at and displayed, with their appearance coded for strong visual and erotic impact...[13]

The notion of the active male and the passive female is made blatant in *Talk to Her* especially through the framing of Alicia and Amparo's naked bodies, particularly Amparo's breasts and pubic area, which act as pure erotic spectacle.

As discussed, the film involves lots of scenes where characters are watching or looking. Mulvey writes that this watching happens on two levels:

> Traditionally, the woman displayed has functioned on two levels: as erotic object for the characters within the screen story, and as erotic object for the spectator within the auditorium, with a shifting tension between the looks on either side of the screen.[14]

Thus, if we are to apply Laura Mulvey's theory to *Talk to Her* it is not only Alfredo, Marco and Benigno who are guilty of looking and objectifying but also us, the spectator. An example of where we, the spectator, look at women from a male point of view is through a series of eye-line match sequences between Marco and Alicia. During one particular sequence at the hospital, Marco is shot in close up peeking round the crack of an open door; the shot cuts to a point-of-view shot of Alicia topless with half of the frame obscured by the door. He is to all intents and purposes a peeping tom. Alicia's pose is different in this scene to much of the rest of the film; her legs are crossed, and she lies slightly on her side with her hand raised like a classical nude in a painting as if she has been posed to be admired (Figs 6 & 7).

During the same sequence Alicia opens her eyes. Benigno says 'That gives me the creeps.' The other nurse says, 'And when she yawns?'; Benigno replies, 'I shit myself.' This could be seen to reinforce the concept of the male gaze. Alicia is there to be looked at. When she opens her eyes

Figs 6 & 7

– i.e. as if she is trying to watch – it is seen as unnatural and scary. Her eyes are quickly closed, thus reinstating the role of male as watcher and female as watched.

It is, however, interesting to note that at several points in the film Alicia's body is filmed from positions where it would be physically impossible to be viewed by the direct gaze of men; i.e. from far above her, to right behind her head. Shots like these could also imply perhaps the camera itself is a naturaly objectifying force rather than it just being males who objectify Alicia.

Interestingly, the male gaze theory was formulated in the 1970s somewhat under the assumption that the film-maker was a heterosexual male eroticising the female body. Almodóvar often explicity mocks and challenges the male gaze in his films. The most notable example of this might be in *Kika*, which begins with a shot looking at a woman through a key hole (literally like a peep show); however, as the film progresses both males and females are seen as voyeurs. The female TV show host Andrea Scarface wears a costume which has fake breasts on show (objectifying herself) but has a camera affixed on her head coding her as a voyeur. It is also worth noting that Almodóvar often objectifies men in his films (*Matador / Tie Me Up Tie Me Down*) and transgender/ transsexual bodies in films such as *Bad Education*.

References

1.	Lebeau, Vicky. (2001) *Psychoanalysis and Cinema: The Play of Shadow*. London: Wallflower Press. p. 2

2.	Lebeau, p. 2

3.	Mackenzie, p. 155

4.	Pedro, Almodóvar (2002) Press Pack www.sonyclassics.com/talktoher/talktoher.pdf. p. 7

5.	Paraphrased from- Gross, Richard. (2001) *Psychology: The Science of Mind and Behaviour*. Kent: Hodder and Stoughton

6.	Wilson, George. M in Edt. Eaton, A.W. (2009) *Philosophers on Film: Talk to Her*. Oxon: Routledge. p. 61

7.	Almodóvar, Pedro. Press Pack.

8.	Paraphrased from www.thefreedictionary.com/psychopath (accessed 28/09/14)

9.	*The Chambers 21st Century Dictionary*. Edinburgh: Chambers. p. 1118

10.	Edt. Strauss, Frederic. (2006) *Almodóvar on Almodóvar*. London: Faber and Faber. p. 213

11.	Meloy, J. Reid. (1998) *The Psychology of Stalking: Clinical and Forensic Perspectives*. London: Academic Press

12.	Zona, M, Sharma, K and Lane, J (1993 Jul;38:4) *A Comparative Study of Erotomanic and Obsessional Subjects in a Forensic Sample*. Journal of Forensic Science. pp. 894-903

13.	Mulvey, Laura. (1975) - *Visual Pleasure and Narrative Cinema*. Screen 16.3 Autumn 1975. p. 10

14.	Mulvey, p. 10

Themes

A theme can be described as a reoccurring idea. Themes tend to be established though either visual or audio motifs and patterns within the narrative. Some of the key themes within *Talk to Her* are loneliness, communication, suicide, faith and age, as could some topics already discussed: the refusal to accept gender stereotypes or gender as a social construct, the body and voyeurism.

Communication

Communication is an integral theme throughout the film. Ironically given the title, the biggest failure in both Benigno and Marco could be said to be their inability to communicate effectively. Benigno talks endlessly to Alicia and has created in his mind the idea that they are a couple; yet, he has never truly listened to her. Similarly Marco's relationship with Lydia begins to break down before her accident due to his own failure to listen. Throughout the film, different modes of communication are explored such as non-verbal and physical communication, miscommunication and misunderstanding, gossip, trash talking, storytelling, **monologue**, **physiognomy**, using music to communicate feelings and the importance of what is left unsaid.

Spoken Communication and Misunderstanding

Robert B. Pippin writes about:

> The deceptive character of spoken conversation, how little gets communicated despite the conversations, especially in comparison to how much can be communicated in silent means.[1]

Perhaps the most obvious incidents of this in *Talk to Her* are in the prison where there are two humorous breakdowns in spoken communication verging on the ridiculous. There is a strange, seemingly superfluous shot as Marco walks in to the prison and asks directions from a male attendant, from whom he gets an efficient response. However, his communication with the next member of staff, who is female, is far from straightforward. They are separated by a glass partition (a reoccurring motif within the film) and filmed in shot/reverse shot. Like Lydia (when she was awake), the woman can hear everything Marco says, but *he* can't hear what she is saying. She says her response again but this time on a comically loud, echoing PA system. For the rest of the conversation she speaks normally and Marco has to strain to listen and concentrate on what she is saying; something he never did with Lydia. The scene ends with the woman again on the loudspeaker informing him that the correct term is 'interns not inmate', implying that even when he has communicated, he has not used the right words. To further emphasise the point, in the next scene Benigno is trying to tell a male prison warden the numbers to dial to reach Marco. The pair fail to effectively communicate and Benigno swears in frustration as they have to start again. George M Wilson states: 'Much of the verbal talking in *Talk to Her* is acutely problematic, a source of distortion, misunderstanding and outright manipulation.'[2]

Monologue

Monologue is one of the modes of communication seen regularly in the film often through story-telling. Monologue is also important during Benigno's therapy session with Dr Roncero. Both men participate in the conversation but, as with Alicia and Lydia, Dr Roncero reveals nothing of himself and instead encourages Benigno to speak. However, Dr Roncero does what neither Benigno nor Alicia can do with each other, which is to ask questions. Traditionally when one thinks of psychiatry we think of lying on a couch and spilling our feelings out to an impartial and passive listener (often from a medical background). Ironically then, during Benigno's 'conversations' with Alicia *she* is the one lying down and Benigno, in his medicalised role, is the one providing the monologue.

The film's title is arguably deceptive. '*Talk to her*' is the kind of advice that one is given when someone is experiencing emotional trouble. One might hear the phrase 'You really need to talk to her, tell her how you feel'; however, with no room for Alicia to communicate back, the title of the film could equally be 'Talk *at* Her' as in reality this is all that Benigno is doing. Almodóvar says of *Talk to Her* that it is '*[a]bout how monologues before a silent person can be an effective form of dialogue*'.[3] Although not effective in literally creating a dialogue (as Alicia can't literally hear Benigno), the monologue is effective in temporarily curing Benigno from his loneliness.

For Marco, monologue is also important. The conversation he has with Lydia in the car is clearly pivotal as it is the only scene to be shown twice:

LYDIA: After the fight we have to talk.

MARCO: We've been talking for an hour.

LYDIA: You, not me.

Marco is equally as unaware of his own lack of communication and, like Benigno, he confuses monologue for dialogue.

Caring as Communication and Storytelling

George M. Wilson states Benigno's understanding of *talking to Alicia* is misunderstood and acts as 'metonymy' (using the name of one thing to actually mean another) 'for the act of taking care of another person with unquestioning love, without any conditions and without any expectations of reward or immediate response.'[4] Just as massaging and washing Alicia is part of his role as a nurse, so too is talking to her. One imagines that Benigno has had very few conversations in his life that do not centre around or take place whilst he is caring for someone and thus it's fair to assume he associates communication with care.

At several points in the film Benigno talks *for* Alicia. When Katerina is describing her ballet Benigno says 'Alicia is loving it'. This could be seen as caring, in that he is personifying and 'including' her in the conversation. One could equally interpret this as more sinister behaviour as he is not only talking *for* her but also imagining her emotions, her likes and personality, something that he has neither the right nor the proper insight to do.

Almodóvar suggests that *Talk to Her*, and his subsequent film *Bad Education*, are celebrations of storytelling:

[Benigno] transforms the ballets he attends into storytelling; and in the first draft, I also had him telling her a whole bunch of films. Storytelling is Benigno's way of surrounding Alicia with everything she used to like before her coma, which as far as he knows is dance and cinema.[5]

But storytelling, as a form of communication, suggests creative licence, imagination and fantasy rather than telling the truth. Benigno's storytelling infantilises Alicia, making her seem like a small child at bedtime. Storytelling also reinforces Benigno's belief that Alicia can hear him, something that neither Marco nor the other nurses believe she can.

What is Left Unsaid

There are several instances where what is not said is of pivotal importance for the plot. Alicia does not tell her father about Benigno's invasion into her room, which would have most certainly dissuaded him from employing Benigno and prevented her rape; but also her awakening. Similarly, Marco is kept in the dark on two occasions about Lydia's affair with El Niño. First by Lydia and then by El Niño himself at the hospital. As a consequence, Marco spends months by Lydia's bedside without knowing of their affair. Similarly, later in the film Marco and Benigno's lawyer choose not tell Benigno about Alicia's awakening from the coma, which could have arguably prevented his suicide. The film ends with more unspoken truths, as Marco does not reveal to Alicia that he knows her. Despite Benigno's last words of advice to not be so secretive, it is ambiguous as to whether Alicia will ever know about her rape and dead baby son.

Non-Verbal Communication

In the Wim Wenders documentary *Piña* (2011), dancer Ruth Amarante, who appears in the penultimate dance of *Talk to Her*, describes how for her, Piña Bausch's choreography was a form of communication: 'Meeting Piña was like finding a language finally. Before I didn't know how to talk and then she suddenly gave me a way to express myself; a vocabulary.'[6]

Dance is the first form of non-verbal communication we are introduced to which also helps to emphasise as Almodóvar puts it, the 'incommunication between couples'[7]. The dancers move without looking at each other, around each other. They run towards but then dodge each other, mirroring the disrupted flow of a conversation where people are talking to each other but not really communicating. Similarly in the penultimate dance the female dancer holds a microphone, but rather than using this as a device to communicate, she breathes into it as if unable to get the words out. In archive footage from *Piña*, Piña Bausch describes how performing Café Müller they had their eyes closed while dancing, thus having to put their complete trust in the male dancer pushing the chairs[8] and rely on other senses rather than sight or spoken word to communicate.

Another example of how non-verbal communication is used both effectively and then less-so in the context of performance is in the bull fighting sequences. First of all, through the various roles and costumes of the bullfighters (or Torero as they are known in Spanish), their status is communicated to the audience. Lydia is a Matador or Matadora de Toros (Female Killer of Bulls). The Matador is the highest position within the bullfight and is signalled visually by her prop; the cape, or The Capote de Paseo. The other Toreros are the Banderillero, who holds banderillas, small flags to be stabbed into the bull's neck. The third torero is the Picador, who rides on a horse and carries a spear. The roles of the Picador and the Banderillero are to tire the bull and to allow the Matador to observe the bull's behaviour before they wave the Capote de Pasero and, in Spanish bullfighting, kill the bull; the *estocada*.

Robert B Pippin likens the struggle to communicate with the bull with, 'the struggle against (silent) animals, brute 'dumb beasts' (snakes and bulls)' with the struggle to communicate with the comatose[9]. During the first bullfight the camera is handheld and tracks in slow motion following the bull. The interaction between Lydia and the bull is like a conversation. Lydia communicates by waving the capote and the bull responds by moving towards her. Lydia is shot from a low angle, making her look masterful – but also slightly manic. In one medium long shot she appears to be standing square on in front of the bull, this time trying to look it in the eye and communicate with it in a more humanistic way. El Niño and his manager comment saying she has 'gone nuts', implying perhaps that trying to communicate with the bull in such a way is impossible.

During the second bullfight, it seems that Lydia, like Marco, is also poor at communicating with the opposite sex. Her male Banderillero and Picador are nowhere to be seen when she is attacked. Lydia seems to take on the seemingly uninjured bull alone without taking the time to observe and learn from its nonverbal communication. Lydia takes a kneeling position; one that even someone with no experience of analysing bullfighting can see is a submissive pose. She is gored. The bull runs from her to a male Banderillero, who communicates more effectively, controlling the bull's movement. The second bullfight is shot in a very different way to the first. Whereas the first ended with a triumphant low angle tracking shot, this fight begins with a high angle tracking shot followed by a much more dramatic high angle long shot, which, despite Lydia's determined facial expression, makes her seem much less threatening. This time we see the scene from the symbolic male perspective of the bull. A bird's-eye view shot of the bull, angrily pacing around its enclosure, cuts to a point-of-view shot from the bull's perspective as it runs aggressively at Lydia. Just as when Benigno rapes Alicia, who cannot communicate with him, so too Lydia has no opportunity to communicate with the bull before it penetrates her. The scene ends on a dramatic close up of the bull looking impassive and unable to communicate.

Communication of the Body: Physiognomy

Almodóvar says of Leonor Watling's body: 'Her motionless body is so expressive and so moving!'[10]

If it weren't for the medical equipment and nurses around Alicia, certain shots of her body could be easily likened to a Victorian erotic photograph or a Pre-Raphaelite nude painting. Looking at the female body as if it were a painting further emphasises the spectacle of the body. Alicia's function is to be looked at and admired. The purpose of the nude in Pre-Raphaelite painting has been speculated to perform several functions, some of which have relevance to Alicia's body. During the Victorian era physiognomy was popularised. Physiognomy is the assessment of a person's character from their outside appearance. For Benigno and Marco, neither of whom have had much (if any) in the way of any other communication with Alicia, the body takes on a greater importance. Benigno believes he is in love with Alicia through her comatose body and the associated, imagined personality he attributes to it. A further reason why Pre-Raphaelite painters painted nudes was a male curiosity with the female body during a sexually repressed time. We assume that Benigno's only experience of the naked female form has been in a medical capacity through his training as a nurse and through the care of his mother. Alicia's body, which is young and would have (at least initially) been toned from dancing, may have been the first body he has experienced which he finds sexually attractive and thus an object of curiosity.

Using Music and Lyrics to Communicate

The first Bullfighting scene is accompanied by a sad love song sung by Elis Regina called 'Por Toda a Minha Vida' which is Portuguese for 'For All my Life'. Like Lydia, Elis Regina died prematurely at the age of thirty-six. The lyrics of the song are about communicating love for one's partner in the form of an oath, a promise and a song:

> Oh! my beloved
> I want to make an oath, a song
> I promise, all my life to only be yours
> and love you like
> Nobody ever loved anybody
> Oh! my beloved, pure star appeared
> I love you and proclaim you
> My love, my love
> More than all that is
> Oh! my love.[11]
> (my translation)

By having a love song accompanying the interaction between Lydia and the bull, one could interpret that Lydia is using the medium of the bullfight to create a grand romantic gesture to prove her love to El Niño. Or, the bull could be symbolic of men in general and the difficulty of communicating emotions between the genders.

Similarly, the lyrics of 'Cucurrucucú Paloma' (the song played during the Spanish Guitar sequence) identifies different modes of communication; 'singing', 'wailing', 'crying'. The lyrics tell a story of a dove (who we assume is symbolic of a man) crying over the departure of an 'unhappy woman'. The story could well be applied to Marco's life as he quite literally begins to cry listening to the song remembering his lost love Angela:

> They say that at nights
> He simply went through by just crying
> They say that he wasn't eating

It simply didn't suit him just taking [some food]
They swear that the sky itself
Was vibrating by listening his weeping
How he was suffering for her,
And even when he was dying he was calling at her:
Ay, ay, ay, ay, ay he was singing
Ay, ay, ay, ay, ay he was wailing
Ay, ay, ay, ay, ay he was singing
He was dying from mortal passion.[12, 13]

Imagined Gossip

As in most of Almodóvar's films, women are associated with gossip as a major form of communication. During a scene at the clinic, the nurses gossip about Benigno and Marco. The subject of the gossip is rude, unrefined and objectifying, as are many conversations between women in Almodóvar's films:

NURSE 1: I love the bullfighter's boyfriend. I bet you anything he's well hung.

ROSA: How do you know? Have you seen him? You want a cookie?

NURSE 1: Of course not. You can tell from a guy's face.

NURSE 2: And especially from his crotch.

NURSE 1: I've got a sixth sense.

Although seemingly superfluous, this scene is important as it depicts conscious women having a crude, gossipy conversation about Benigno and Marco as opposed to the imagined conversation that that Benigno suggests that the comatose Alicia and Lydia are having about them on the balcony. During the balcony scene Benigno positions the women in such a way as they appear to be facing each other, each of them in sunglasses with dressing gowns and scarves wrapped around their waists presumably to keep them upright (Fig. 1). The effect is somewhere between two women on holiday lounging on sun chairs next to a pool or two Japanese Geishas.

Fig. 1

Considering the two as Geishas is interesting. The word 'Geisha' literally means 'performing artist', which Alicia and Lydia both were. Like Alicia, Geisha's are often trained in dancing. Although modern Geishas are strictly entertainers, the Geisha has, at points within its history, been associated with the courtesan and prostitute, meaning that even today modern Geishas are sometimes, like Alicia, confused for objects for sex. Like the comatose women, who could be said to operate in a different world to the rest of the characters, Geishas are said to inhabit *Karyūkai* ; the flower and willow world, one steeped in ritual, mystery and tradition. Just as Geishas often live in women-lead communities, interestingly all the patients in comas that we see or are mentioned are women. At the end of the film, Benigno takes sleeping pills in an attempt to put himself in a coma and enter this imagined world.

Benigno says of Alicia and Lydia: 'It's like they were talking about us. What do you think they'd talk about? Women tell each other everything.' Unlike the crude conversation of the nurses who really do tell each other everything, even if Lydia and Alicia were awake, it is likely that their conversations about Benigno and Marco would not be the 'girly crush' conversation that Benigno imagines. Lydia might well say she is bored of Marco while Alicia might recount the tale of the creepy man who snuck into her room. But as they are unable to communicate, the scene emphasises their isolation and the men's lack of understanding about what true female communication would sound like.

Trash Talk and Chatter

Almodóvar is also fascinated with women 'trash talking' and as such gives a fairly insignificant character, Dr Roncero's receptionist, one of the funniest lines in the film. 'I've just taken an elephant sized dump,' she tells a friend on the 'phone, while belching and yawning uncouthly. But she is a model of a real woman; shitting, burping and talking crudely, she is utterly unlike the fairytale Sleeping Beauty princess that Benigno imagines Alicia to be.

Similarly the character of Lydia's sister, although appearing briefly, offers a model of chatty conversation that the central characters do not experience. She starts off telling an anecdote about nuns in Africa who were raped by priests.

SISTER: Did you hear about the nuns? The ones who were raped by the missionaries in Africa... The priests themselves! It's horrible If you can't trust a missionary what is to become of us?

MARCO: They used to rape the locals.

SISTER: Really!?

MARCO: Because of Aids they started raping the nuns.

SISTER: Oh my God! And I had missionaries on a pedestal.

LYDIA'S MANAGER: I'm sure not all of them are rapists.

ANTONIO: No, some of them are paedophiles.

SISTER: What's that?'

The conversation takes a comedic turn when her husband Antonio reduces the seriousness of the conversation by saying 'everyone loves fucking'. What's intriguing about this conversation is that, despite its superficially irreverence and irrelevance (albeit, rape-related), it offers a model of effective group conversation that cannot be found with the central four characters. It focuses on a topic of general interest, all four people are involved, the tone is light and humorous and the characters are both listening and responding.

Small Talk

Small talk is an interesting, yet minor aspect of communication within the film. There are several moments of irrelevant small talk that are used between Benigno and the other nurses. The first,

> BENIGNO: Washing her hair?
>
> MATHILDE: What does it look like?

paints Benigno to be a poor conversationalist who states the blatantly obvious as a conversational opening gambit. The second demonstrates a more important point about women and real conversation:

> ROSA: God it's so hot... I bought something in the drugstore to help stop the perspiration stains on my uniform. Your armpits don't sweat but the rest... look at my face.
>
> BENIGNO: What's it called?
>
> ROSA: Oh God!... Perspirex.

This conversation is very much in Almodóvar's style as many of his films include reference to fictional products. For example, his very first film *Pepi, Luci, Bom* contained adverts for imaginary products such as a pair of knickers that soak up urine. Again, this is another example of women proving that they are real. Unlike the body of Alicia, which seems to be kept in a clinical state of constant washing, oiling and massaging, Rosa is a real woman with all-over sweat problems!

Suicide as a Form of Communication

All three suicides in the film can be interpreted as forms of communication. On first viewing of *Talk to Her* there appears to only be one suicide – Benigno's – but on second watching one can interpret two more suicides.

Muñoz interprets Lydia's goring to be 'an inexplicable suicide attempt [...] the act of desperation from a misunderstood woman' due to the way that Lydia takes on a submissive kneeling pose with little hope of defeating the bull.[14] Lydia's suicide could be seen as a public display of exasperation. During the earlier bullfight the following conversation happens between

El Niño and his manager foreshadowing her later 'suicide'.

EL NIÑO: She's gone nuts

MANAGER: She's dedicating it to you ... she'd let that bull tear her apart just so you could see... We shouldn't have come, especially you.

She is isolated; unable to be heard by Marco, enduring a troubled relationship with El Niño and now cannot communicate effectively with the bull.

The third event that can be considered a suicide is Alfredo's entrance to Amparo's vagina in 'The Shrinking Lover'. Clearly it would be impossible (not to mention fairly dark, dull and unhygienic!) to live in Amparo's vagina thus, Alfredo can be thought to kill himself. Alfredo's suicide can be thought of as an act of romantic or erotic communication or perhaps an admission that he has reached the pinnacle of all he is likely to achieve in his tiny state. This suicide can be interpreted as playing on the phrase 'le petit morte' – 'the little death' – which is an idiom for an orgasm. Alfredo's suicide could be a literal interpretation of this idiom; a little death from a little man dying during an act of sexual climax.

Benigno's suicide can in some sense not be considered deliberate, as his intention was not to die but to be left in a coma like Alicia. Rather, Benigno's suicide is an attempt to enter the mystery world of a coma, where he hopes he might be able to communicate with Alicia. In prison he is denied a voice (as his lawyers do not understand his point of view) and he can no longer speak to Alicia, so his suicide can be thought of a desperate step towards what he hopes will be a state where he will be able to communicate again.

Themes: Age and Paedophilia

Benigno and Alicia are coded as a younger couple (early twenties) whereas Marco and Lydia appear older (mid-thirties). Older characters such as Katerina and Dr Roncero (mid-fifties) are placed in parental roles. On first viewing of the film, age seems like a fairly irrelevant theme; however, when one re-watches and analyses scenes again, age becomes more of a problematic issue, made even more apparent when one considers the casting choices.

Throughout, the spectator is given clues as to how old the characters are within the film. For example, when asked what he knows about women, Benigno states that he had been with his mother for twenty years and caring for Alicia for four implying that he is meant to be twenty-four. However, the date on his tombstone reads 16/6/1972, which would make him thirty (if we assume the film is meant to be set in the year of its release, 2002). Furthermore, the actor Javier Cámara was born in 1967 making him thirty-four at the time of filming. Benigno appears childish due to his naivety, chubbiness and performance, but close ups of his face make him seem older. There is little about him that places him at the age of twenty-four and indeed, in her analysis of the film, Ira Jaffe describes Benigno as a 'relentlessly hopeful man, perhaps forty years old, hitherto a virgin'.[15] Alicia, by contrast, is much easier to place in terms of age. We assume from her appearance and the fact she still lives at home that she is somewhere between the age of eighteen to twenty-two; or possibly, and potentially more disturbingly, younger. Indeed, on the website for the film Almodóvar describes Alicia as being an adolescent.[16]

During the scene when she is raped, Benigno appears to have done Alicia's hair and makeup in such a way that she looks paradoxically childish *and* womanly; a Lolita figure. Her hair is in pigtails with pink ribbons on the end and a pink bow clip; the way a mother might arrange a little girl's hair for school. She wears pink lipstick and pale eye shadow, but no mascara or eyeliner; it is the kind of make up a very young teenager might apply before going to a party. This raises some interesting questions. Does Benigno want to dress Alicia as a child because he himself is childlike, thus making his obsession with Alicia more like a teenage crush? Or, more disturbingly, when one considers the actors' real age, is he a grooming predator sexually aroused by young girls?

Secondly, there is also the insinuation that Marco has had a relationship with a very young girl. At the wedding Lydia comments on how young Angela looks and indeed, the actress who played her, Elena Anaya, was twenty-seven when the movie was shot in contrast to Darío Grandinetti (Marco) who was forty-three during the filming. Marco claims he has not been in a relationship with Angela for ten years and prior to that, they were in a relationship for five years. If we assume that Angela and Marco are meant to be roughly the same age as the actors playing them (twenty seven and forty three) that would make Angela twelve and Marco twenty-seven at the start of their relationship. Despite the fact that the age of sexual consent is thirteen in Spain, the age difference between them adds a potentially disturbing dynamic to their relationship.

To declare Marco and Benigno paedophiles would be too simplistic an assumption, but upon closer inspection of age within the film, their preferences are definitely suspicious. C.D.C. Reeve says of Benigno and Marco's taste in younger women:

> Inside Benigno, there is something black, something that leads him to have sex with a comatose woman. Inside Marco, there also seems to be something black, something that smells bad, whatever name we choose to give it.[17]

For Benigno who is infantilised and naïve, a real woman of his own age would be potentially threatening. Perhaps he considers himself childlike and innocent; after all, he says of himself 'I'm harmless'. For Marco who claims to be an expert in desperate women, his role in previous relationships, like Benigno, may also have been of carer. But, whereas Benigno spent much of his life caring for an older woman (coding him as child), Marco appears to have had a relationship effectively caring for a younger woman (coding him as father figure). When Marco finds an age appropriate partner in Lydia he is unable to communicate with her effectively, perhaps implying that he has been used to a more one-sided relationship with a troubled adolescent rather than an adult female who could be his equal.

Themes: The Impossibility of a Relationship[18]

In very few of Almodóvar's films are there many models of effective relationships between men and women, and many of his films, such as *The Flower of My Secret*, are about the break-up of relationships more than the formation of them. In the few films where romances are formed, they tend to end badly, sometimes spectacularly so. Annette Guse, in analysing the collaboration between Almodóvar and Piña Bausch, identified that a similar theme in both of their work is that of the 'impossibility of relationships between man and woman.'[19] In the opening dance sequence this is made most apparent as the two women and the man dance around each other almost connecting but never quite.

Although not present in the excerpt from Cafe Müller dance, the full choreography goes on to explore the difficulties of romance. A woman hugs frantically at a man whilst another man pulls her off repeatedly.

Perhaps Almodóvar's rejection of functioning relationships within his films echoes his own experiences of relationships as a homosexual man. Perhaps his conception of romantic relationships between men and women is grounded in his own lack of personal experience of a heterosexual relationship. That said, there are few examples of functioning *homosexual* couples in his films either, with dysfunctional homosexual relationships depicted in *Law of Desire* and *I'm So Excited!* In *I'm So Excited!* Almodóvar depicts a marriage whereby a husband (the pilot) is having an affair with a (male) member of the cabin crew, and discovers his wife is having a lesbian affair; yet the relationships seem to function because of, rather than despite, their apparent dysfunctionality.

All around the central characters of *Talk to Her* there are broken relationships, some by death, in the case of Alicia's parents, and some by separation, in the case of Benigno's. As Despina Kakoudaki suggests, the only functioning relationships in the film are the 'potential relationships' (that of Alicia and Marco) and the 'fantasy relationships' (the one that Benigno imagines he and Alicia have).[20]

Benigno and Marco are initially represented as keen to help the women of broken relationships. The first such relationship we come across is of fellow nurse Mathilde, whose husband has walked out on her. Benigno, like Marco, seems used to caring for desperate women and offers to cover her shifts saying 'Look, your husband walked out on you and the kids, you do the nights you can and I'll do the rest, between us we will manage.' The second woman from a broken relationship is Lydia who has recently broken up with El Niño. Marco is equally willing to help out.

In amongst these broken relationships there is one couple that seem to have it sorted and yet they only have a very small role in the film. Lydia's sister is her opposite in many ways. She is much more traditionally feminine; more curvaceous, caring and affectionate. She and her husband fulfil much more traditional gender roles than many of the other characters in the film. Her husband, whom she calls 'a brute', is physically large and typically masculine in appearance. After Lydia's goring, the camera zooms out from her sister's face as she cries looking blankly into the distance. Her husband holds her affectionately. A title comes up, 'Three weeks later'. Lydia's sister is still crying and still being held by her husband. This time they are leaving the hospital. Lydia's sister says she would like to stay for longer but cites one of the reasons why she cannot is that 'I have neglected this man', referring to her husband. This couple seem to understand each other and respect the need to pay each other attention. What is the implication here? Is it that only those couples that follow traditional gender roles can have successful relationships? Perhaps this is also strengthened by the implication that Marco, the more traditionally masculine of the two male leads, and Alicia, who is arguably the more traditionally feminine female lead, will embark on a relationship.

Relationships as Performance

One could argue that the film positions relationships as pretence and performance. The chat show host cynically suggests Lydia and El Niño's relationship was a performance, as she says 'Do you think it was all just a show to promote himself? [...] A man who shared not just fame and the bullring but your bed as well'. Later when Marco meets her in the bar and offers to drive her to Madrid, there is a small moment where, as they are walking past El Niño, Lydia puts her arm through Marco's (who is clearly taken aback), the first instance of pretending they are a couple. Yet despite Marco's presence in her life, El Niño remains a constant figure. When Marco kills the snake in the side of the frame there is a picture of Lydia and El Niño together; even his act of heroism cannot replace her ex- lover's presence in her life. Later, in the hotel room, the *mise-en-scène* strengthens the theme of performance with the motif of a red silk curtain behind Marco and Lydia echoing the curtain that lifted before the initial dance sequences (Fig. 2). They could be interpreted as being actors behind stage about to go on in front of their audience.

Themes: Loneliness

Talk to Her is a story about the friendship between two men, about loneliness and the long convalescence of the wounds provoked by passion.[21]

Fig. 2

Rather than telling Lydia that he is single, Marco instead hesitates and says, 'I'm alone'. He uses the same phrase after finding out of Lydia's affair with El Niño, telling Alicia, 'I'm alone again'. The word 'alone' seems to have a weight of sadness attached to it that the phrase 'I'm single' doesn't. Similarly, during the scene in Dr. Roncero's office, Benigno confesses that he is lonely. When asked why he's in therapy he says 'Loneliness, I guess'. In the self-interview used to promote the film, Almodóvar suggests that 'Loneliness, I guess' would have been another possible title for it.[22]

Benigno lives alone, goes to the cinema alone and appears to have few friends. Despite the fact that many of the characters are physically together, they are essentially alone. Marco and Lydia are alone in their failure to communicate effectively. Alicia and Benigno are alone in their contrasting states of unconsciousness and consciousness. Even the surrounding characters appear to be alone. Katerina appears to be single, as does Rosa and Dr. Roncero.

Loneliness is a theme that Almodóvar has returned to throughout his career. Many of his films feature single women or women who are isolated within marriages, such as in *What Have I Done to Deserve This*. They also feature people who are unable to connect with others often due to their upbringing, such as Angel in *Matador*. In many of Almodóvar's films such as *Pepi, Luci, Bom* and *Women on the Verge of a Nervous Breakdown*, women come together as an antidote to loneliness. Alicia and Lydia are forced into an unconscious kind of loneliness but, unlike Almodóvar's other characters, they cannot form a female community in which to counteract their isolation. Whilst not physically alone, they are mentally isolated and are unable to feel the loneliness that their state forces on those around them.

Marco has a potentially lonely career. He is a travel writer and thus has to go to foreign countries alone. While most adults travel in couples or groups, Marco is shot in extreme long shot on a beach in Jordan emphasising how isolating his job is. Indeed, when Lydia first meets Marco he is drinking alone in a bar hoping to catch an interview with her.

Fig. 3

Loneliness is established through the props in Benigno's jail cell. Marco gives Benigno some travel books and Benigno says he was moved by the description of the people in Havana. On the front cover of the book on Cuba is a woman who, like Benigno used to do, looks out from a balcony (Fig. 3). He talks about how the Cuban people invent things; perhaps, in a small way he is beginning to realise that he has invented his relationship with Alicia. He says:

> BENIGNO: I really identify with those people; who've got nothing and invent everything. When you describe that Cuban woman leaning out a window by the Malecón waiting uselessly, seeing how time passes and nothing happens... I thought that woman was me.

Almodóvar says that 'Cinema is the refuge of loners'.[23] One could argue that the whole act of watching a film is a lonely pursuit as spectators sit in darkened rooms, watching but not communicating. The theme of loneliness could potentially be inspired by Almodóvar's own life. Almodóvar is a celebrity in Spain who has gone to great lengths to keep his private life out of the media. As such, it is uncertain as to whether he is in a relationship or is alone. He is homosexual and unmarried (same-sex marriage in Spain has been legal since 2005) and is famous for having close platonic relationships with his actresses, notably Penelope Cruz; but, he, like the characters in his films, is potentially lonely. He says in an interview with Frederic Strauss that he, too, uses cinema as a refuge and 'I am more solitary than I used to be'.[24]

Themes: Faith

There are conflicting representations of faith in *Talk to Her*: those who have it, those who are losing it and those for whom faith conflicts with their scientific point of view. To add to this there are also different types of faith: religion, superstition, belief in miracles and devotion to another person as a kind of faith.

The Catholic Church was of the utmost importance to the Franco regime with catholic values and worship part of the Spanish way of life. After Franco's death, democracy brought with it increased secularisation. Almodóvar grew up as a catholic and attended a school where he studied under Salesian Priests in training to become a priest but he is now not a practicing catholic. Throughout his career Almodóvar has held both a fascination with the Catholic Church and also a desire to poke fun at it, which he did most notably in *Dark Habits*, about a group of nuns who take heroin amongst a cocktail of other drugs.

Faith and superstition are tied together within *Talk to Her*. Before each bullfight Lydia's sister lights candles in a shrine supposedly for luck. Similarly, Lydia kisses her medals, which act as a talisman. Later in the hospital, when Marco asks when they can be put back on, an extreme close up focuses on the medals, which appear to show the Virgin Mary. Marco says, 'She never took them off'. Clearly, the medals are not lucky as Lydia has been gored, but they, and the shrine, demonstrate the style of Catholic faith that relies on symbols, objects, ritual and tradition. Almodóvar writes about how for him, religious iconography is tied up with a 'kitsch aesthetic'.[25] This is notable in Lydia's hospital room. In the shrine, her sister has remade the makeshift collage of postcards of photos. The shrine is similar to the tacky, portable Hindu shrine that air host Fajas carries with him in *I'm So Excited!* As Lydia's sister lights candles again, this time to pray for Lydia's recovery, she admits that she is 'finding it hard to have faith'.

Benigno has a faith that is not necessarily religious, but is fuelled by his love for Alicia. Benigno believes in miracles and encourages fellow nurse Rosa to do so too. Benigno is even willing to act upon his faith; so strong is his belief that Alicia will wake up that he decorates his flat in a style similar in colour scheme to her bedroom in her family home. He also believes, without any proof, that Alicia can hear him; perhaps in the way that people might pray and speak to God without any proof that they are being listened to.

Marco's conversation with Dr Vega establishes the difficulties those from a scientific background have with faith:

> MARCO: How long can Alicia stay like this?
>
> DR VEGA: Months, years, her whole life.
>
> MARCO: Is there any hope?
>
> DR VEGA: As a Doctor I have to say no... However...

Dr Vega presents Marco with a (fictional) magazine article about Meryl Lazy Moon who went into a coma after the birth of her third child and awoke after 15 years. The conversation continues:

> DR VEGA: Her recovery contradicts all I am about to say.
>
> MARCO: So that means there is hope?
>
> DR VEGA: No, I repeat, scientifically no. But if you choose to believe, go ahead.

Despite the strong elements of coincidence and presence of a 'miracle' (Alicia's awakening) within the narrative, *Talk to Her* grounds itself in reality through the inclusion of medical discussion, medical procedures and iconography of medical charts, making Alicia's awakening from her coma plausible and suspending the audience's sense of disbelief throughout the film. Dr. Vega demonstrates the complex position which those with a scientific background face; having faith despite a weight of scientific evidence against doing so.

Themes: Privacy and Spectacle

Almodóvar says that '*Talk to Her*' tells a private, romantic, secret story, peppered with independent spectacular units'.[26] As he explains moments of privacy can be misunderstood for moments of spectacle. For example he says:

> When Benigno sees [Alicia] dance for the first time (from the window opposite) he doesn't hear the music. Alicia seems to be absorbed in an interior melody.[27]

For Alicia her dance practice is personal, 'interior' and private; she does not know she is being watched. For Benigno it is like a performance, one which he watches with rapt attention.

Alicia's breasts are often displayed during the film in a way that is sometimes spectacle. During the scene at Alicia's house, upon leaving her bedroom, Benigno bumps into Alicia who has just got out of the shower. She screams as she covers herself to keep her breasts hidden from him. Her embarrassment heightens how inappropriate Benigno and Marco's treatment of her breasts is at other points in the film. For example, Marco enters the room and talks to her while she lays on her side with her breasts uncovered. Rather than cover her up and respect Alicia's right to privacy, Benigno enters and says to him crudely 'admit it you were looking at her tits'.

Lydia's privacy is challenged by the media during the talk show scene. During the shot where Lydia is being taken out of the bull ring after being gored, a low angle shot, as if from Lydia's point of view, shows a camera pointed straight down at her taking a photo; a photo that would be grotesque both in its image and its invasion of her privacy (Fig. 4). This kind of invasion is seen in other Almodóvar films, notably *Kika* where Kika's rape is broadcast on TV. These media invasions are perhaps informed by Almodóvar's own experience of his private life being invaded by the Spanish press. Later in *Talk to Her*, this press invasion is parodied and poked fun at by Benigno's concierge who is annoyed that the media have not come to interview her about his imprisonment.

Fig. 4

References

1. Pippin, Robert B in Eaton, A.W. (2009) *Philosophers on Film: Talk to Her.* Oxon: Routledge. p. 38

2. Wilson, George. M in Edt. Eaton, A.W. (2009) *Philosophers on Film: Talk to Her.* Oxon: Routledge. p. 46

3. Almodóvar, Pedro. Self-Interview www.sonyclassics.com/talktoher/flashwebsite/core/hasFlash.html (accessed 29/09/14)

4. Wilson, p. 48

5. Almodóvar, Pedro in Edt. Strauss, Frederic. (2006) *Almodóvar on Almodóvar.* London: Faber and Faber. p. 215

6. Ruth Amarante. *Piña* (2011 dir. Wim Wenders)

7. Almodóvar, Pedro. Self-Interview www.sonyclassics.com/talktoher/flashwebsite/core/hasFlash.html (accessed 29/09/14)

8. Piña Bausch. *Piña* (2011 dir. Wim Wenders)

9. Pippin, in Eaton, p. 38

10. Almodóvar, Pedro. Self-Interview www.sonyclassics.com/talktoher/flashwebsite/core/hasFlash.html (accessed 29/09/14)

11. *Por Toda a Minha Vida.* Antonio Carlos Jobim (as Tom Jobim) and Vinicius de Moraes. Arapua Editora Musical (Brasil)

12. *Cucurrucucú Paloma* Tomás Méndez

13. Interestingly, although both songs sound very Spanish to the English ear, *Por Toda a Minha Vida* is Brazilian Portuguese in origin and Cucurrucucú Paloma is Mexican in origin but sung by a Brazilian Singer, Ceteano Veloso. Mexican, Spanish and Brazilian Portuguese would all be understood by a Spanish audience but the languages have slight subtle differences. This adds another problematic issue communication into the film through the understanding of different languages. Notably, Marco is also Argentinian which has its own slightly different variation of the Spanish language.

14. Acevedo-Muñoz, Ernesto R. (2007) *Pedro Almodóvar.* London: British Film Institute. p. 245

15. Jaffe, Ira (2008) *Hollywood Hybrids: Mixing Genres in Contemporary Films.* Plymouth: Rowan and Littlefield. p. 155

16. Almodóvar, Pedro. www.sonyclassics.com/talktoher/flashwebsite/core/hasFlash.html (accessed 28/09/14)

17. Reeve, C.D.C in Edt. Eaton, A.W. (2009) *Philosophers on Film: Talk to Her.* Oxon: Routledge

18. Guse, Annette. (Nov 2007, Vol. 43 Issue 4) *Talk to Her! Look at her! Pina Bausch in Pedro Almodóvar's Hable con Ella.* Journal of Germanic Studies. p. 427

19. Guse, p. 427

20. Kakoudaki, Despina in Edt. Epps, Bradley and Kakoudaki, Despina. (2007) *All about Almodóvar: A Passion for Cinema.* Minneapolis: Minnesota University Press. p. 221

21. Almodóvar, Pedro. Self-Interview. www.sonyclassics.com/talktoher/flashwebsite/core/hasFlash.html (Accessed 29/09/14)

22. Almodóvar, Pedro. Self-Interview

23. Almodóvar interviewed in Strauss, Frederic. (2006) *Almodóvar on Almodóvar.* London: Faber and Faber

24. Strauss, p. 228

25. Strauss, p. 35

26. Almodóvar, Pedro. www.sonyclassics.com/talktoher/flashwebsite/core/hasFlash.html (accessed 29/09/14)

27. Almodóvar, Pedro

Genre and Narrative

Narrative

Ernesto Acevedo-Muñoz says of narrative in Almodóvar's films that they seem to be 'stories in search of a format, always on the verge of spinning out of control, but finally held together by their own aesthetic, generic and formal rules'.[1] *Talk to Her*'s narrative shouldn't work. It flits between a double- and single-stranded plot line, it plays with time with sometimes careless abandon and contains coincidences that verge of the ridiculous. But yet, far from alienating the spectator, the narrative of *Talk to Her* pleasingly draws one in and lures the spectator into a position where they are able to suspend their disbelief, enjoy and engage with the plot. As Muñoz states, it seems to be within the consistent instability of Almodóvar's narratives that one can find stability[2]. In other words, the spectator familiar with Almodóvar's films somewhat expects an unconventional narrative and thus is likely to find it unobtrusive.

The Narrative of Spain

Thomas Sotinel likens the at times chaotic narrative structures of Almodóvar's films to the chaos and instability of Spain's past. While most of his work, including *Talk to Her*, is set in the present day, Sotinel argues that there is constant allusion to Spain's troubled history under Franco.[3] Similarly, Muñoz states: 'Ultimately, the essence of Almodóvar's aesthetics has always been [...] the desire to make logic out of chaos and to rebuild the family and the nation out of its own fragmentation and the trauma of the past'.[4] *Talk to Her* can be thought of as a story of rape and rebirth, which are themes central to Spain's past. Aurora G. Morcillo suggests, as others have, that Spain is often gendered as female and that 'The concept of 'nation' turns into the physical figure of a 'woman' with all the attendant qualities- nurturing, vulnerability, fertility'.[5] Thus, one could interpret the narrative as being an **allegory**; Franco's dictatorship (as male) can be thought of as the symbolic rape of a country (as female); penetrating its culture and values by force. Alicia's 'rebirth', her awakening from a coma, and to a certain extent Marco's 'rebirth' into a man who has potentially learnt how to communicate, can be likened to the post-Franco cultural movement La Movida Madrileña in which Spain itself can be considered to be 'reborn' both culturally and in terms of gender roles and relations.

Rejecting Traditional Narrative Structures

Due to the double stranded narrative of Alicia and Benigno and Marco and Lydia, it is hard to place *Talk to Her* within any classic narrative structures such as those developed by **Propp** or **Todorov**. As with many of Almodóvar's films, much of the narrative relies on coincidence. For example, it is a coincidence that Marco sits next to Benigno during the dance performance at the start of the film and then later ends up meeting Benigno in the hospital; and it is a coincidence that Marco and Alicia meet each other at the end of the film. Although the film does build to a climax somewhat reminiscent of a thriller (e.g. a crime is committed and a perpetrator found and prosecuted) the editing never quite builds to a state in which the spectator could experience tension as it might in a Hollywood film. Equally, there are no clear binary opposites within the film. Marco never quite makes it as a heroic protagonist as he is flawed in his inability to communicate effectively and Benigno is arguably treated too sympathetically to be thought of as a true **antagonist**.

Cycles

Talk to Her could be described as cyclical in its narrative with plots playing out with the hint that scenarios might reoccur. This is most notable in the scene where, after Benigno's death, we see Marco in Benigno's flat watching Alicia from the window. This mirrors an earlier scene where Benigno is filmed in a near identical mid shot and eye-line match sequence. The implication might be that Marco will develop a similar obsession with watching Alicia. Further to this, the non-diegetic title 'Marco y Alicia' at the end of the film also suggests that a relationship will be formed between the two as the narrative device of non-diegetic titles appeared earlier in the film with the title 'Marco y Lydia', introducing his previous relationship. The final shot of the film features two dancers nervously flirting and slowly shuffling towards each other; symbolic perhaps of Alicia and Marco. While, to a certain extent, the film achieves narrative resolution, there could well have been a second film made after this about the complexities and ambiguities of Marco and Alicia's potential relationship. Would Marco tell Alicia about Benigno and her pregnancy? How would she react if he did? What would Katerina's reaction be to the relationship? Just as the last words of the film are 'nothing is simple' so too the ending of the film is filled with complexity and ambiguity.

Time

Time in *Talk to Her* is dealt with in a non-linear fashion; in the press pack Almodóvar describes it as 'as lineal as a rollercoaster'.[6] We jump forward and backward through time as we follow Benigno and Marco's stories; however, for Alicia and Lydia, as Almodóvar states, time stands still he speaks about the 'suspended time between the walls of the clinic'.[7]

The very beginning of the film at the dance performance is, we realise later, a flashback as Benigno is telling Alicia about the performance. This sets the tone for a narrative structure that uses frequent flashbacks and relies on reflections and stories about the past. The film continues chronologically for a time as Marco and Lydia meet; however, the film somewhat ignores any development in Marco and Lydia's relationship by using the title 'Several months later', perhaps implying that the relationship has developed without due care and attention from Marco and thus is also obscured from the spectator. The titles used throughout help to frame scenes and allow the spectator to gain a sense of temporal orientation in an otherwise potentially confusing chronology. In the following scene Lydia is gored by the bull and taken to hospital now in a coma. The next scene we are presented with is at first unclear; while enjoying a performance of Spanish guitar music there is a close up of Lydia's face. The spectator at this point might question whether she has made a recovery but in fact this is a flash back to before the accident and presumably, because of Lydia's affection towards Marco, before her affair with El Niño. What follows next is a flashback *within* a flashback as Marco recounts the tale of the snake in Angela's tent while she and Marco were in Africa. Interestingly, this time, rather than cutting to the flashback, the scene is superimposed on the background next to the close up of Marco perhaps to avoid confusion or perhaps to make a point about memory and how one can be in the present but still be affected by and remember ones past (Fig. 1). The next shot shows Marco waking up in the present in

Fig. 1

hospital, raising questions about what we have seen; a true objective flashback? A dream? Or a subjective memory?

As with Benigno's previous flashback, the next flashback is told as a story with a voiceover. This time, however, the listener is Marco not Alicia, as Benigno unashamedly recounts the tale of his obsession with Alicia and his journey to becoming her nurse. Again, within the flashback the passage of time is dealt with strangely and we get little sense of how long the events have taken place over. Has his obsession with Alicia lasted for weeks, months or even years? From first talking to Alicia to arranging an appointment with her father, has he waited hours, days or weeks? We are given certain clues, such as a shot of Benigno at the window fading to black and then fading back into the same shot but with Benigno now dressed in a different outfit, suggesting perhaps that his voyeurism is a regular occurrence.

During the flashback, the narrative device of foreshadowing is employed. As Alicia crosses a busy street, the camera is placed on the pavement watching her rush between the cars, possibly forewarning her impending accident. The scene ends back in the hospital room where Marco, seemingly unperturbed by the story, listens as Benigno continues to massage Lydia. According to Almodóvar: 'Broken time and a mixture of various narrative units works best when the action is more mental or interior.'[8] The film as a whole can be said to be much more character-driven and thus 'mental' or 'interior' than much of the action-driven narratives of Hollywood films. Almodóvar states that in *Talk to Her* he 'plays with time' in a way in which he rarely does so much in other films. Perhaps this is natural given that the film involves four central characters and takes place over the course of years. Similarly, backstory is important in the film in helping us understand characters. Flashbacks are used to give us small insights in Benigno's life with his mother and what Dr. Roncero refers to as his 'special upbringing', and Marco's turbulent relationship with the young and fragile Angela.

Collage, Dance and Music

Sotinel argues that *Talk to Her*, as with Almodóvar's earlier *Labyrinth of Passions*, is a 'collage' rather than a rigid structured narrative.[9] However, as opposed to being completely random he states that 'it all fits together harmoniously and you can't even guess where the joins occur'. Unlike a true collage film which, in the style perhaps of Dziga Vertov's *Man With a Movie Camera* (1929) would be narratively reduced by the editing to montage, *Talk to Her* can be considered collage in the number of micro stories and moments within the narrative that embellish rather than progress the plot; 'The Shrinking Lover', the wedding scene involving of Marco's ex-girlfriend Angela, the dance sequences and the Spanish guitar sequence.

Concurrently, parts of *Talk to Her* could be considered poetic through sequences like the slow motion bull fighting and through the use of music and dance as narrative devices. Almodóvar states that through her choreography, 'Piña Bausch had unknowingly created the best doors through which to enter and leave *Talk To Her*'.[10] The two dance sequences could be seen to act as a **prologue** and an **epilogue** to the film, as the movements and interactions between male and female dancers echo the themes within the film of the active and the passive female and also mirror the relationships between the women and the men who fail to effectively communicate.

Alongside dance, music is interesting to consider in terms of its place within the narrative. Around half way through the film there is a scene lasting around four minutes which just consists of a crowd of people watching a performance of *Cucurrucucú Paloma* played on the Spanish guitar by Ceteano Veloso. The scene does little to develop the plot but instead, like the on screen audience, the spectators of the film are invited to pause, to watch and to 'be' for a few minutes before the narrative progresses. This device is used in several other Almodóvar films, notably *Dark Habits* where fallen from glory pop singer Yolanda Bell performs for the nuns. Muñoz refers to such narrative interruptions as 'a place where paradoxically 'real emotions' can be glimpsed and where characters often confront real feelings'.[11] This is certainly true for Marco, who cries whilst watching the performance. Muñoz further suggests that the narrative role of such sequences act as 'emotional juncture', referring to it in the context of a character's emotions, but one could equally interpret these sequences as acting as a juncture for the *spectator* to explore feelings and emotions.[12]

Media interlude

Muñoz coins the term 'Media interlude'[13] to refer to sequences within Almodóvar's films where he uses other films, TV shows or plays as narrative devices to draw comparisons to the characters situations such as the use of the Tennessee Williams play *A Streetcar Named Desire* (1947) in his previous film *All About My Mother*. The most obvious example of a media interlude is that of 'The Shrinking Lover' sequence, which uses cinema and the medium of film itself as a narrative device. Unlike some of Almodóvar's films that reference existing films, such as *Matador* which includes a scene where the central characters visit the cinema and watch *Duel In The Sun* (1946), *Talk to Her* creates its own film, referencing the silent cinema era, early body horror films and B-movies of the 1950s. Almodóvar states:

> For me, the films I see become part of my own experiences, and I use them as such. There's no intention of paying homage to their directors or of imitating them. They're elements which are absorbed into the script and become part of it. 'Telling films' is something that has to do with my biography.[14]

Thus, the inclusion of films and cinema within his films acts on two levels: firstly, in, as he states being 'absorbed into the script' in a thematic or symbolic way; and secondly, in the case of 'The Shrinking Lover', acting as an 'interlude' from the main narrative by following another smaller narrative – literally a story within a story. In his self-interview in the press materials for *Talk To Her*, Almodóvar refers to the sequence as a 'lid' and explains how he uses film as a narrative device to manipulate:

Q: *What is the reason for the detour of the main story?*

A: The story does not stop, it melts. In any way, when I was writing the script, it was so that the mute film served as the lid.

Q: *The lid for what?*

A: The lid to cover what is really happening. I do not want to show the viewer.

Q: *That is called manipulation.*

A: It is a narrative option, and not an easy one, but I am happy with the result.[15]

As the opening shot of the sequence begins with a dissolve from the movie poster of 'The Shrinking Lover' to the hospital, this 'lid' idea is made literal as the image of 'The Shrinking Lover' is for a moment explicitly overlaid on top of Alicia and Begnino's story.

Watching and Re-watching

Interestingly, Cynthia Freeland suggests that the complexities of *Talk to Her* cannot be fully appreciated upon first viewing and the film has to be re-watched to fully analyse and engage with it. This is an interesting approach as this style of watching arguably goes against the tradition of narrative film as cinematic medium and suggests it should be analysed in the same way as a book or a painting; in chapters or over time. Freeland suggests that '*Talk to Her* calls for its audience to grasp its basic message by reviewing, re-watching and reinterpreting scenes we saw earlier and found innocuous'.[16] This might suggest that the film calls for the spectator to take scenes out of their narrative context and analyse them as fragments rather than as a whole. This opens a wider question about the intention of narrative and film as a medium, whether it is cinematic and meant to be viewed in the dark for the full running time of 108 minutes[17] uninterrupted or whether, in the age of the DVD, that the spectator can actively engage with parts of the film, re-watching and thus experiencing scenes and characters in a way which was not initially intended when considering the narrative as a whole.

Genre

Q: *What genre does Hable Con Ella belong to?*

A: All I know is that it is not a Western or a CIA agent's movie. It is not a James Bond or period movie either.

Q: *It does have a bit of period in it...*

A: It is true, 7 minutes that take place in 1924.[18]

Like most Almodóvar films, *Talk to Her* is hard to classify in terms of genre. Unlike the Hollywood system that relies heavily on either star or genre marketing, the marketing for Almodóvar's films relies heavily on his own status as an award-winning auteur film-maker. *Talk to Her* is thus not bound by generic convention in the way that many Hollywood films are. Acevedo Muñoz defines Almodóvar's 'genre instability' to be a defining characteristic of his work, and he goes on to say that this instability might echo further instability within Spain as a whole. Muñoz states that the crisis of genre and narrative identity in Almodóvar's films is akin to 'national and individual identity crises, the trauma of Spain's past and the parallel treatment of political and sexual repression'.[19]

From the 1920s Hollywood cinema created a model of genre-based production with certain studios specialising in specific genres (such as MGM specialising in musicals). While today movie studios are much more diverse in the genres they produce, the importance of genre remains due to it its benefit for both producers (in marketing) and audiences (in making viewing choices). Spanish cinema has never had such a heavily industrialised system of film production as the US and as a consequence has never had such a strong tradition of genre cinema. Consequently, Almodóvar has not been obliged to follow genre structures and conventions in the way a Hollywood director might.

Whilst Almodóvar had no formal university training in film, he is well understood to be a cinephile and his reference, parody and pastiche of

Hollywood melodrama is present in many of his earlier films. Like other directors who could be considered as both **cinephiles** and auteurs, such as Quentin Tarantino or Wes Anderson, Almodóvar is able to select, reject or bend genre conventions. Unlike other successful non-American directors, such as the French Luc Besson, fellow Spaniard Alejandro Amenabar or Mexican Guillermo Del Toro, who have all worked in Hollywood, Almodóvar has remained resolutely Spanish and therefore has not had to bend to the demands of the Hollywood genre machine.

Almodóvar's international audience, which could be described as a predominantly cinephile, art house crowd, has also made it easier for Almodóvar to create films that do not fit into a clear genre. The genre of his films for this audience could be 'Almodóvarian', i.e. that his status as a director in and of itself offers potential distributors and spectators the same marketability and recognition as Hollywood genre films albeit for a more niche audience.

As Thomas Sotinel writes, 'Almodóvar is unable to limit himself to one single point of reference' and as such, one can interpret *Talk to Her* as adhering to contentions from multitude of genres.[20] Furthermore, Allinson and Jordan write:

> [Almodóvar's films] remain generic hybrids, i.e. impure, carnivalesque, textual constructs, a 'collage' bearing the traces of earlier styles and genres which often clash.[21]

Thus, in the following pages we shall consider how *Talk to Her* borrows conventions from several different genres.

Thriller

On the surface, *Talk to Her* could be made to sound like a thriller: An obsessed loner, who lives with his mother, stalks an unsuspecting dancer. He becomes her nurse, rapes her, is imprisoned and then kills himself. However, the film lacks enough conventions to truly convince as a thriller, mainly due to the brightly coloured *mise-en-scène*, high key lighting and comedic elements. The film also fails to create an adequate amount of tension to be viewed as a thriller. The spectator response for a thriller is to be thrilled and *Talk to Her* does not achieve this; it instead demands an intellectual response from the viewer. Like a psychological thriller, we, like a thriller film detective, try to analyse and unravel the Benigno's behaviour. However, in psychological thriller there is normally little sympathy or likeability of the antagonist, which arguably the viewer experiences in relation to Benigno.

Noir

The film could be thought of as having some elements of a film noir, particularly in the convention of having a flawed central male protagonist being draw into a web of ethical quandary and crime. Noir films frequently end miserably, ambiguously or, as is the case in *Talk to Her*, with the imprisonment and/or death of the central protagonist. However, it's hard to see how Benigno fits the archetypal noir protagonist of a hard-boiled detective or patsy to a *femme fatale*. Equally it's impossible to consider Alicia in such a role. To see Alicia as someone who seduces the protagonist is ethically challenging as it implies Alicia in her comatose state is capable of seduction. Again, the vibrant colour palette of *Talk to Her* also seems to go against the idea of it being fully considered a noir film as such films are typified by a monochrome colour palette and chiaroscuro lighting.

Romance

The title of the film could be interpreted as sounding like a romance or rom-com alongside other films with similar titles such as *What Women Want* (2000) and *Just Go With it* (2011). These titles seem to offer advice about relationships. The non-diegetic titles 'Marco y Lydia', 'Benigno y Alicia' and then later 'Marco y Alicia' all help to frame these pairs as romantic couples. While the spectator understands that Alicia and Benigno are *not* a romantic couple, Benigno's belief in the relationship is so strong that they are coded as a couple

Interestingly, the marketing of the film focused on the two women rather than representing the men and women as couples. In reality this makes little sense as Alicia and Lydia never meet in the narrative except in a comatose state, but it suggests that Almodóvar was keen for *Talk to Her* to not be interpreted as a romance.

Tamar Jeffers McDonald defines the romantic genre as 'A film which has as its central narrative motor a quest for love, which portrays this quest in a light hearted way and almost always to a successful conclusion.[22] Marco and Benigno could be interpreted somewhat as on a quest for love and both are romantic souls, if unorthodox. The film is light hearted in some senses, through some of the dialogue, but the film gets progressively less so in tone towards the conclusion. Furthermore, the lack of a traditional romantic resolution arguably makes *Talk to Her* less of a romance according to Jeffers McDonald's definition.

Whilst there is arguably less identifiable iconography within the romantic genre than other, more visual genres, Erica Todd highlights the importance of objects and symbols within the genre when she states:

> In Hollywood romantic dramas [...] the love is so intense that it lives on through memory, nostalgia and the symbols that remain as effigy after the demise of the relationship.[23]

For Benigno, Alicia's hairclip takes on board a strong significance as fitting with Todd's assertion. Without any other objects in which they share a common experience, the hair clip takes on added meaning. Benigno takes it to prison with him and is buried with it.

Buddy Movie

Ironically, given its female-centric marketing, the film could also be described as a buddy movie; a story about friendship that survives against significant adversity. Indeed in IMDb.com's description of the film – 'Two men share an odd friendship while they care for two women who are both in deep comas'[24] – male friendship is highlighted rather than rape or romance. Buddy movies often involve two people (usually male) with clashing personalities who are forced together by circumstance. Buddy films are light-hearted and often end with the two men finding a common ground. Perhaps the marketing avoided the depictions of Marco and Benigno due to the subtle **homoerotic** undertones that could be interpreted in a film with two sensitive and emotional men as its central protagonists, which might deflect from the preferred reading of the film.

Drama and Melodrama

The genre which is both perhaps most fitting but also most broad is that of drama. Drama films are defined by character-lead as opposed to action-lead narratives. There are no natural disasters, alien attacks or superheroes in *Talk to Her* to make the narrative progress. Other than the car accident and the goring which cause the comas, all of the other progressions within the narrative are a result of characters' actions and emotions. Many of Almodóvar's films have been described as being in the drama subgenre of melodrama. Melodrama is a genre most identified with 1950s films targeted at women which focus on relationship issues and typified by stylised performances, domestic settings and heightened emotion. While many scenes in *Talk to Her* adhere to these conventions, the fact that the central protagonists are male and the female characters are in a vegetative state for most of the film, subverts the female-centric nature of melodrama. Yet Muñoz highlights melodramatic conventions used in the film, such as the iconography of rain and its association with emotion and the use of the hospital location, suggesting that these conventions make the more fantastical elements of the film (such as Alicia's reawakening) plausible and believable.[25]

Tragicomedy

A tragicomedy is a hybrid genre of film that mixes tragedy (suffering) and comedy (humour). Benigno's imprisonment and suicide, and indeed his whole life, could be considered tragic. Lydia's desperation and death could equally be regarded as tragic. The sad orchestral soundtrack that accompanies Benigno's imprisonment by composer Alberto Iglesias seems to accentuate the tragedy in Benigno's life. The comedy within the film comes through the dialogue and also through the absurdity of 'The Shrinking Lover' sequence. Almodóvar describes this scene in relation to tragicomedy: 'The tone is comic but there's an epic dimension to it too'.[26]

Ira Jaffe suggests that Beningo is 'the film's chief comedian' and that 'comedy features as much as any other genre in *Talk to Her*'. She refers to dialogue such as that in the clinic where Benigno 'presents himself as an authority of the feminine mystique'.[27] It is important to consider comedy in this context as not necessarily provoking a laugh-out-loud kind of response but as being light-hearted or funny in an absurdist/unusual way.

Silent Cinema and Postmodernity

While *Talk to Her* in its entirety could hardly be described as a silent film, it is important to consider the genre conventions present in 'The Shrinking Lover' sequence (see the in-depth analysis in 'Messages and Values: Rape and Moral Ambiguity'). Apart from the obvious black and white colour palette there are some other important conventions such as intertitles, melodramatic performances and make-up. Because of his genre reflexivity, Almodóvar has been often referred to as a postmodernist director. Postmodernism is about the breakdown in eras and styles and in divisions between high and low art. *Talk to Her* encompasses both the high art elements of contemporary dance with the low art form of TV chat shows, and modern day film-making with that in the style of the silent era. In a sense, Almodóvar's appropriation of so many different generic elements renders the concept of genre as crucial but simultaneously irrelevant in discussion of his films.

References

1. Muñoz, Ernesto Acevedo. (2007) *World Directors: Pedro Almodóvar*. London: British Film Institute Acevedo. p. 1

2. Muñoz, p. 2

3. Sotinel, Thomas. (2010) *Masters of Cinema: Pedro Almodóvar*. Paris: Cahiers Du Cinema Sarl 11

4. Muñoz, p. 4

5. Morcillo, Aurora G. (2010) *The Seduction of Modern Spain: The Female Body and the Francoist Body Politic*. Massachusetts: Rosewood Publishing and Printing Corp. p. 13

6. Almodóvar, Pedro. (accessed 03/08/2014) *Pepe and the Narrative* www.sonyclassics.com/talktoher/flashwebsite/core/hasFlash.html

7. Almodóvar, Pedro. (accessed 03/08/2014) *Pepe and the Narrative* www.sonyclassics.com/talktoher/flashwebsite/core/hasFlash.html

8. Sotinel, p. 79

9. Almodóvar, Pedro (accessed 03/08/14) www.sadlerswells.com/pina-bausch/pedro-Almodóvar-talks-about-pina-bauschs-influence-on-his-films

10. Almodóvar, Pedro (accessed 03/08/14) www.sadlerswells.com/pina-bausch/pedro-Almodóvar-talks-about-pina-bauschs-influence-on-his-films

11. Muñoz, p. 17

12. Muñoz, p. 169

13. Muñoz, p. 162

14. Almodóvar, Pedro. (accessed 03/08/14) *Talk to Her* Press Pack www.sonyclassics.com/talktoher/talktoher.pdf

15. Almodóvar, Pedro. (accessed 03/08/2014) Self Interview www.sonyclassics.com/talktoher/flashwebsite/core/hasFlash.html

16. Freeland, Cynthia 'Nothing is Simple' in Eaton, A.W (2009) *Philosophers on Film: Talk to Her*. Oxon: Routledge p. 71

17. The Region 2 DVD has a running time on 108 minutes but the press pack says it has a running time of 112 minutes

18. Almodóvar, Pedro.(2002) *Talk to Her* Press Pack www.sonyclassics.com/talktoher/talktoher.pdf.

19. Muñoz, p. 62

20. Sotinel, p. 29

21. Jordan, Barry and Allinson, Mark (2005) *Spanish Cinema a Student's Guide*. London: Hodder Arnold. p. 81

22. Jeffers McDonald, Tamar.(2007) *Romantic Comedy: Boy Meets Girl Meets Genre*. London:Wallflower Press. p. 9

23. Todd, Erica. (2014) *Passionate Love and Popular Cinema: Romance and Film Genre*. New York, Palgrave Macmillan

24. http://www.imdb.com/title/tt0287467/ (accessed 09/09/14)

25. Muñoz, p. 260

26. Edt. Strauss, Frederic. (2006) *Almoóvar on Almodóvar*. London: Faber and Faber. p. 260

27. Jaffe, Ira (2008) *Hollywood Hybrids: Mixing Genres in Contemporary Films*. Plymouth: Rowan and Littlefield. p. 155

Audience and Critical Response

There is no one clear target audience for *Talk to Her* in the way that there might be for a Hollywood rom-com or fantasy film but, the film can be thought of as roughly **positioned** to: An audience familiar with Almodóvar, middle aged, middle class, liberal, predominantly European, cultured cinephiles who are interested in films that get good reviews and films that have won awards.

The film can be thought to appeal to fans of Almodóvar and in this sense, whilst Hollywood often uses **star marketing**, the distributors of Almodóvar's films often position Almodóvar as the star. Almodóvar's star marketing is particularly important in marketing the film abroad with the posters and trailers of the film saying 'a film by Almodóvar' prominently. The release of *Talk to Her* in Spain and France coincided with an exhibition of photographs and a large-scale billboard campaign in Madrid and then Paris in conjunction with the shop FNAC, a music, film and book retailer. The campaign focused around Almodóvar as a **cult figure**.

Marvin D' Lugo suggests that in his early career Almodóvar had 'consciously cultivated the image of a celebrity auteur'.[1] One could compare this to Hitchcock who became such an iconic figure that he was sometimes more famous than the stars of his films. D'Lugo states:

> [Almodóvar's] strategy was to construct what amounted to a media image of the film-maker as celebrity through his performance art, writings, and cameo appearances in his films.[2]

Almodóvar uses the cult figure status he has refined in the promotion of *Talk to Her*. This is noticeable in the press pack and website self-interview for *Talk to Her* in which he literally interviews himself about the film (essential reading for anyone studying the film). Thus one gets an insight into Almodóvar's view of his own film in a way in which one rarely gets in such depth from other directors. Furthermore, several books have been published which focus primarily on interviews with Almodóvar such as *Almodóvar on Almodóvar* (ed. Strauss, 2006) and *Pedro Almodóvar Interviews* (ed. Willoquet-Marcoprinti, 2004). On the official website for the film, Almodóvar goes into depth analysing his own films and gives background details on some of the characters which one wouldn't know from simply viewing the film. Almodóvar is thus positioning himself as a director who wants people to actively analyse his work and take different interpretations from it.

In terms of age, the film is likely to have been positioned to a middle aged audience due to the controversial subject matter and complex narrative. The film was given a 15 Classification by the **British Board of Film Classification** for the following reasons:

> Three subtitled uses of 'fuck' and the gory sight of a character injured during a bullfight along with references to bestiality, rape, coprophilia, menstruation, paedophilia, homosexuality, suicide (by implied ingestion of Valium) and similar 'mature' themes, required a 15 under the BBFC Guidelines at that time. However, there were also some additional issues – sex references, sexual violence and possible animal cruelty. [...] The sexually abusive relationship Benigno forms with his patient was also felt to be containable at 15, not least as the film clearly condemns this behaviour. [3]

The BBFC report is definitely worth reading as it gives an interesting account of how rape is presented and interpreted by the audience. It also investigates how the film, which uses real injured bulls, was able to get round animal cruelty laws in the UK. (Note that bull fighting is legal in Spain but illegal in the UK.)

Classification globally varied hugely from being a U in France (suitable for all) to a 12 in Spain, an R in the US (meaning children under 17 are not allowed to see it at the cinema unaccompanied), an R 18 in the Philippines (meaning that no one under the age of 18 is allowed to view it) and even an R21 in Singapore (meaning no one under the age of 21 is allowed to see it).[4] This says a great deal about the film's ability to work on two levels; a surface level where violence and sexual violence are hidden from the spectator and on a deeper level whereby Benigno can be viewed as a sinister stalker, rapist or even necrophiliac.

The film was popular in its native Spain opening in 276 screens, making $1 million in its opening weekend and $6,089,345 overall. However, as Sally Faulkner states Almodóvar is a 'transnational director' and he has a relatively large following abroad.[5] Marvin D'Lugo refers to his 'geocultural positioning' and says:

Fig. 1 - Talk to Her *DVD cover, which boasts the same artwork and typography as the theatrical release poster.*

His style has gradually evolved to the point that when we speak of 'a film by Almodóvar', though rooted in a specific Spanish cultural reality, it is also designed to circulate internationally.[6]

Whilst it is unlikely that outside of Spain *Talk to Her* would have had a **wide blanket release**, the film had reasonable success abroad. In other **film territories**, the film would have likely been considered by exhibitors and distributors as having a niche, art house audience. As such, it was screened mainly at independent cinemas and art house cinema chains such as Curzon in the UK.

Increasingly, studios release those films they identify as having major awards potential in November–December prior to the awards season, beginning in January with the Golden Globes. *Talk to Her* was no exception with a December release in the US. During this time period, cinemas are filled with 'quality films', often within the genre of drama, all vying for award success. This also says something about the target audience in the US where the film made $9,285,469, 18% of its total worldwide gross of $51,001,550. The type of audience for subtitled dramas in the US are most likely cinephiles; well educated, cultured, liberal and interested in films that get good reviews. They are most likely to live in cosmopolitan cities particularly on the East and West coasts.

The film was also particularly popular in France making $9,264,928 compared to the relatively small $1,345,280 made from UK audiences. France, a nation of cinema-goers, is often more receptive to both art house cinema and European cinema than UK audiences, many of whom prefer English language cinema originating from the US. According to the UK Film Council Statistical Yearbook, in 2002 European cinema accounted for a tiny 0.7% of the UK box office share.[7] During 2002 *Talk to Her* was the third highest grossing foreign film after *Devdas* (India) and *Y Tu Mama Tambien* (Mexico).

In classifying the film's audience in terms of gender, Almodóvar is often thought of as a woman's director in that he celebrates women and often features women as his central protagonists. However, it would be deceptive to think that this makes his audience solely female as some of his films, such as *Kika* and *Tie me Up! Tie me Down!* (and arguably *Talk to Her*) offer real challenges to a feminist spectator due to their depictions of rape, female subjugation and voyeurism. Equally, Almodóvar often depicts men as being deeply flawed, sexually deviant, disturbed and obsessive.

Almodóvar is sometimes thought of having an LGBTQ following in his celebration of different sexualities. However, *Talk to Her* is somewhat of a departure, focusing as it does on two heterosexual 'couples'. Thus, regardless of gender or sexual orientation, *Talk to Her* is most likely to appeal to people with liberal attitudes and, in particular, liberal attitudes towards gender and sexuality in its continual rejection and renegotiation of traditional gender roles.

Critical Reception and Audience Response

Overall the film received resoundingly positive critical acclaim receiving 92% positive reviews according to the review aggregator Rottentomatoes. com[8] and 86% positive reviews on the aggregator Metacritic.com.[9]

Reviewing the film for the BBC, Tom Dawson described it as: 'an effortlessly accomplished and richly resonant work […] a film of exceptional compassion and generosity',[10] while Total Film described it as 'Touching, melancholic and deeply haunting'[11] and Sight and Sound included it in the included it in their top 30 films of the first decade of the millennium.

Critics were mainly positive about the complex narrative, in line with the fact that it won Best Original Screenplay at the Oscars. Matthew Turner, in Empire Magazine, wrote: 'The script, [...] makes excellent use of a free-flowing, flashback structure that allows us to get to know [the women], albeit through the eyes of the male narrators.' [12] Similarly José Arroyo, writing in Sight and Sound, commented:

> Somehow [Almodóvar] can take morally and emotionally difficult subject matter and make something familiar and new: a supremely complex story, simply told, which conveys a range of feeling at once precise and endlessly evocative.[13]

Many critics have praised Talk to Her as being a turning point in Almodóvar's career. In a review of the film for The New York Times, Elvis Mitchell wrote that Talk to Her was the result of a '...superb filmmaker at the grown-up peak of his powers'.[14] Similarly Peter Bradshaw of the Guardian writes that the film reflects Almodóvar's status as an auteur:

> Almodóvar's new movie is calmer and less floridly extravagant, less wired than many of his previous films. Yet every frame bears his signature: the theatricality, the mischievously effective suspense, the adventures in identity and sexuality. It's the most unmistakable auteur flourish in modern European cinema.[15]

In researching for this chapter, it's really important to note that wholly negative reviews were very hard to come by in the quality press. There was more criticism from those writing online in blogs and forums. Often, however, even those who found Almodóvar's message troubling tended to be impressed by his technical expertise. Writing for the San Francisco Gate, Mick LaSalle wrote: 'To be sure, Almodóvar wants to disturb audiences, but is he aware of the misogyny and sexual panic blaring like a siren from the screen?'[16]

Similarly, Alex Sandell of the review site Juicy Cerebellum admired the technical skills of the film but was appalled by its message:

> I feel more like the film is a cleverly designed piece of propaganda created to help a person overcome any feelings of guilt that he or she may have over committing a repulsive crime of hate. [...] Talk to Her crosses the line from 'morally ambiguous' to 'morally depraved,' and no amount of technical proficiency or clever story-telling can

save it. I would sincerely like to recommend this film for its beautiful cinematography, delightful acting, touching moments of subtlety and its wicked sense of humour. Still, there have been a handful of well-made films that I could never recommend to anyone due to their message, just as I won't recommend *Talk to Her* to anyone now.[17]

Most critics enjoyed the 'Shrinking Lover' sequence, the Australian critic Louise Keller described it as: 'a stunning pivotal sequence that shocks, amuses and entertains in a bewildering way'[18] However one reviewer for the The Chicago Reader described the sequence as 'gratingly pretentious'.[19] Similarly, whilst the vast majority of critics enjoyed the inclusion of choreographies by Piña Bausch, J. Hoberman of The Village Voice described the ending as being a 'lurch [...] toward the closure of another terrible, or at least, terribly shot, Bausch presentation'.[20]

Whilst reviewers like Phillip French for the Observer described the film as 'warm and humane',[21] some bloggers and audience reviews found the work lacked emotional impact:

> His stories leave me cold, not caring about or believing in the characters.[22]

> I appreciate his films, and I even love certain aspects of them, but in the end they feel too slight to me. *Hable con Ella* is the same, as I appreciated much of it but when the movie had finished I felt unfulfilled.[23]

References

1. D'Lugo, Marvin. (2006) *Contemporary Film-makers: Pedro Almodóvar*. USA: University of Illinois Press. p. 7

2. D'Lugo, p. 7

3. www.bbfc.co.uk/case-studies/talk-her (accessed 21/09/14)

4. Imdb.com (accessed 21/09/14)

5. Faulkener

6. D'Lugo, p. 2

7. BFI Statistical Yearbook 2002. www.bfi.org.uk/sites/bfi.org.uk/files/downloads/uk-film-council-film-in-the-uk-2002-statistical-yearbook.pdf. p. 14

8. www.rottentomatoes.com/m/talk_to_her/reviews/ (accessed 21/09/14)

9. www.metacritic.com/movie/talk-to-her (accessed 21/09/14)

10. www.bbc.co.uk/films/2002/08/08/talk_to_her_2002_review.shtml (accessed 21/09/14)

11. www.totalfilm.com/reviews/cinema/talk-to-her (accessed 21/09/14)

12. www.empireonline.com/reviews/ReviewComplete.asp?FID=8252 (accessed 21/09/14)

13. José Arroyo, S&S September 2002 old.bfi.org.uk/sightandsound/feature/49593 (accessed 21/09/14)

14. www.nytimes.com/movie/review?res=9B02E5D8153AF931A25753C1A9649C8B63 (accessed 14/08/14)

15. Bradshaw, Peter. (Friday 23rd August 2002) *Talk to Her* www.theguardian.com/film/2002/aug/23/1 (accessed 19/09/14)

16. La Salle, Mick (Wednesday, December 25, 2002) www.sfgate.com/movies/article/Holiday-Movies-Acts-of-undying-devotion-2743536.php (accessed 19/09/14)

17. www.juicycerebellum.com/200255.htm (accessed 19/09/14)

18. Keller, Louise. www.urbancinefile.com.au/home/view.asp?a=7074&s=Reviews (accessed 19/09/14)

19. Jones. J.R. www.chicagoreader.com/chicago/talk-to-her/Film?oid=1070352 (accessed 19/09/14)

20. Hoberman, J. www.villagevoice.com/2002-11-19/film/roads-to-hell/2/ (accessed 19/09/14)

21. French, Phillip. (Sunday 25 August 2002) *Coma Versus Coma* www.theguardian.com/film/2002/aug/25/philipfrench (accessed 19/09/14)

22. www.billsmovieemporium.wordpress.com/2014/02/02/this-week-in-cinema-january-26-february-01-2014/ (accessed 19/09/14)

23. www.imdb.com/reviews/337/33722.html (accessed 19/09/14)

Summary

Talk to Her is a film that reflects the social and historical context of Spain and demonstrates many of Almodóvar's auteur characteristics. Its award winning screenplay defies traditional conventions in genre and narrative structure whilst still creating something that is aesthetically pleasing and accessible to view. The interpretations cited in this book are not the only interpretations. This is a film which becomes richer through discussion and analysis and by approaching it from different critical approaches such as: auteur, genre, narrative, gender and psychoanalytic film theory.

The film leaves the viewer with many interesting questions to consider: How do you feel about Benigno at the beginning of the film and how do you feel afterwards? How do you feel about the fact that Alicia wakes up as a direct consequence of rape? Is Lydia a victim, a liar or a desperate woman? Is Marco the film's hero or just as morally defective as Benigno? Is Begnino a victim or a villain? Do the films aesthetics make its ethics more challenging to consider? Is Alicia better off not knowing what happened to her or does she have the right to know? How does the film reflect Spanish social history? Is the film genreless and how might this affect our expectations?

It is also be important to look at the film within the body of Almodóvar's work particularly through looking at his depictions of rape in *Kika*, *Matador*, *The Skin I Live In* and *I'm so Excited* amongst others. One could also compare *Talk to Her* to any of his other films in terms of gender studies and the representation of men and women. *Talk to Her* could be seen to fit into a more mature phase in Almodóvar's career. With this in mind, it may be interesting to compare his earlier films such as *Pepi Luci Bom*, which was heavily influenced by the hedonism of La Movida, to his later films (from *The Flower of my Secret* onwards) which are arguably more complex and thought provoking.

One could also compare *Talk to Her* with other films that deal with communication and unconventional 'relationships' such as *Her* (2013) which sees a man fall in love with his phone operating system or *Lars and the Real Girl* (2007) where a young Ryan Gosling falls in love with a sex doll. Films that deal with voyeurism such as *One Hour Photo* (2002), *Peeping Tom* (1960) or the Hitchcock films *Rear Window* and *Psycho* may also prove to be interesting comparisons. *Talk to Her* quite clearly draws upon Spanish cultural iconography and thus it would be interesting to compare it to films by other Spanish directors such as Luis Bunel, Alejandro Amenábar, Bigas Lunas and, more recently, Pablo Berger (director of *Blancanieves*).

Glossary

The following words and phrases are highlighted when first mentioned in the text of *Studying Talk to Her*.

Allegory – a story about one thing that is really about something else.

Androgyny – the combining of male and female characteristics to create gender ambiguity.

Antagonist – the villain.

Apolitical – not political, or politically neutral.

Auteur theory – the theory that particular film-makers (usually directors) have signature characteristics that reoccur throughout their work.

Binary opposites – two opposing forces that come together to create a conflict in the narrative.

Bird's-eye view shot – a shot taken from directly above a subject/setting.

British Board of Film Classification (BBFC) – the organisation that certificates films in the UK.

Cinematography – camera framing, angles and movement.

Cinephiles – avid cinema goers/film watchers/those who study and analyse film.

Colour palette – the main colours used within a scene.

Communist – a political philosophy whereby property is owned by the state and distributed according to need.

Corporeality – the nature of the physical body.

Cult figure – a personality/public figure held in high regard by a particular group of people.

Dialogue – lines of script between two or more people.

Diegetic sound – sound that the characters within the text can hear, part of the internal world of the film.

Editing – the cutting and arranging of shots together.

Epilogue – a separate short section after the main narrative that normally summarises some of the themes and issues of the main story.

Eye-line match – the first shot is of a face looking at something; the second shot is of what the character is looking at.

Film Festival – an event where new and classic films are screened to critics, distributors and, sometimes, the public.

Film territories – the country/groups of countries that a distributor will own the rights to distribute a film within.

Gender progressive – open-minded ideas about gender and gender roles.

Genre – a way of categorising films that are similar in style/storyline.

Government subsidy – when the government helps to fund a project through grants or tax breaks.

Hedonism – a school of thought where pleasure is valued above all else.

Homage – to pay respect to another artist/genre.

Homoerotic – concerning sexual arousal between people of the same gender.

Hyper-reality – an exaggerated form of something real.

Iconography – the visual symbols associated with a country, a genre, a religion or an era.

Ideology – the dominant ideas of a group or society.

Intertextual – where the film references other media texts, such as films, books or TV shows.

Kitsch – something which is understood to be in bad taste but is ironically popular (often used to describe interior décor, e.g. flying ducks/ garden gnomes).

LGBTQ – Lesbian, Gay, Bisexual, Transgender/Transexual, Queer.

Liberal – open minded and progressive.

Melodrama – a subgenre of drama that focuses on female, character-driven narratives often in domestic settings with themes of romance and coincidence.

Mise-en-scène – the visual elements in the scene such as costume, hair, setting and lighting.

Monologue – lines of script said by just one person often in the form of storytelling or a speech.

Motif – objects, symbols, sounds or colours that reoccur in the film often to create meaning.

Narrative – the storyline and how it is structured.

Necrophilia – sexual attraction to dead bodies.

Non-diegetic – sounds like music and voice-overs that the characters within the text cannot hear but the audience can.

Non-diegetic title/text – text that cannot be seen by the characters that helps the spectator to understand something about the scene.

Pan – camera movement to the side.

Parody – to mock the genre or work of another artist through copying its style.

Pastiche – to imitate the style of a director or genre.

Patriarchal – male lead/dominated.

Physiognomy – the assessment of a person's personality by just looking at their appearance.

Point-of-view – a shot as if from the perspective of a character.

Positioned – the demographic at the marketing for the film is targeted.

Press pack – the materials distributed at film festivals and press screenings to help promote the film.

Prologue – a separate section before the main narrative that normally reflects some of the themes and issues of the main story.

Propaganda – media designed to spread a political and often biased message.

Propp's narrative theory – the proposition that all narratives are made up of certain 'stock' characters such a hero, villain, princess, donor, dispatcher, false hero and the princess's father.

Protagonist – the hero (often the main character).

Reoccurring tropes – commonly used scenes, themes or characters.

Representations – how groups of people, events or places come across/ are portrayed in the text.

Scopophilia – obtaining sexual pleasure from watching.

Shallow focus – when the foreground is in focus but the background is out of focus.

Shot in sequence – when a film is shot in the order that the events appear in the film.

Shot/reverse shot – when the shot cuts from one subject/character and reverses the shot to see another subject/ character; often used in conversations.

Star marketing – promotion that focuses on the stars as the main tool in attracting an audience.

Subculture – a smaller culture within the mainstream (see also: Cult figure).

Symptomatic *mise-en-scène* – a visual arrangement that allows us to understand character's personalities.

Stanislavsky method – where actors try to learn and experience everything about their character's life, not just what the script tell them.

Theme – a reoccurring topic or idea within the film.

Todorov's narrative theory – the idea that all stories follow broadly the same narrative structure: equilibrium, disruption, recognition, repair, new equilibrium.

Voyeurism – spying on people, often with a sexual connotation.

Wide Blanket Release – when a film is released to a large number of cinemas on the same day, often at the same time around the world.

Bibliography

Books

De Beauvoir, Simone (1949) *The Second Sex*. Paris: Editions Galimard.

D'Lugo, Marvin. (2006) *Contemporary Film-makers: Pedro Almodóvar*. USA: University of Illinois Press.

Eaton, A.W (2009) *Philosophers on Film: Talk to Her*. Oxon: Routledge.

Edt. Epps, Bradley and Kakoudaki, Despina. (2007) *All about Almodóvar: A Passion for Cinema*. Minneapolis: Minessota University Press.

Faulkner, Sally. (2013) *A History of Spanish Film: Cinema and Society 1910-2010*. London: Bloomsbury Academic.

Gross, Richard. (2001) *Psychology: The Science of Mind and Behaviour*. Kent: Hodder and Stoughton.

Jaffe, Ira (2008) *Hollywood Hybrids: Mixing Genres in Contemporary Films*. Plymouth: Rowan and Littlefield Meloy, J. Reid. (1998) *The Psychology of Stalking: Clinical and Forensic Perspectives*. London: Academic Press.

Jeffers McDonald, Tamar.(2007) *Romantic Comedy: Boy Meets Girl Meets Genre*. London:Wallflower Press.9.

Jordan, Barry and Allinson, Mark (2005) *Spanish Cinema a Student's Guide*. London: Hodder Arnold.

Julian Smith, Paul. (2014) *Desire Unlimited: The Cinema of Pedro Almodóvar*. London: Verso.

Lannon, Francis. (2003) *The Spanish Civil War, 1936-1939*. Oxford: Osprey Publishing.

Lebeau, Vicky. (2001) *Psychoanalysis and Cinema: The Play of Shadow*. London: Wallflower Press.

Mercer, John and Shingler, Martin. (2004) *Melodrama, Genre, Style, Sensibility*. London: Wallflower Press.

Morcillo, Aurora G. (2010) *The Seduction of Modern Spain: The Female Body and the Francoist Body Politic*. Massachusetts: Rosewood Publishing and Printing Corp.

Paula Willoquet-Maricondi. (2004) *Pedro Almodóvar: Interviews.* USA University Press of Mississippi.

Sotinel, Thomas. (2010) *Masters of Cinema: Pedro Almodóvar.* Paris: Cahiers Du Cinema Sarl.

Edt. Strauss, Frederic. (2006) *Almodóvar on Almodóvar.* London: Faber and Faber. Russell, Dominique. (2010) *Rape in Art Cinema.* London: The Continuum International Publishing Group.

The Bible: contemporary English version (2000). London: Harper Collins.

The Chambers 21st Century Dictionary. Edinburgh: Chambers. 1118.

Todd, Erica. (2014) *Passionate Love and Popular Cinema: Romance and Film Genre.* New York, Palgrave Macmillan.

Zona, M, Sharma, K and Lane, J (1993 Jul;38:4) *A Comparative Study of Erotomanic and Obsessional Subjects in a Forensic Sample.* Journal of Forensic Science.

Websites

www.bbc.co.uk/films/2002/08/08/talk_to_her_2002_review.shtml

www.bbfc.co.uk/case-studies/talk-her

www.billsmovieemporium.wordpress.com/2014/02/02/this-week-in-cinema-january-26-february-01-2014/

www.culturecourt.com/F/Latin/TalkToHer.htm

www.imdb.com/reviews/337/33722.html

www.juicycerebellum.com/200255.htm

www.metacritic.com/movie/talk-to-her

www.rottentomatoes.com/m/talk_to_her/reviews/

www.sadlerswells.com/pina-bausch/pedro-Almodóvar-talks-about-pina-bauschs-influence-on-his-films

www.sonyclassics.com/talktoher/flashwebsite/core/hasFlash.html

www.urbancinefile.com.au/home/view.asp?a=7074&s=Reviews

Magazines and Newspapers

Chritina Sanchez, quoted in Adela Gooch Saturday 22 May 1999 Bullfighter gored by male rivals www.theguardian.com/world/1999/may/22/1

www.rollingstone.com/movies/reviews/talk-to-her-20021105 (accessed 10/09/14)

www.filmmakermagazine.com/ archives/issues/spring1994/pedro.php#.VBCxAPldXwg

Woodward, Adam. (23rd August 2011) *Pedro Almodóvar* www.littlewhitelies.co.uk/features/articles/pedro-almodovar-16259

www.chicagoreader.com/chicago/talk-to-her/Film?oid=1070352

www.villagevoice.com/2002-11-19/film/roads-to-hell/2/

www.theguardian.com/film/2002/aug/25/philipfrench

www.totalfilm.com/reviews/cinema/talk-to-her

www.empireonline.com/reviews/ReviewComplete.asp?FID=8252

José Arroyo, S&S September 2002 old.bfi.org.uk/sightandsound/feature/49593

www.nytimes.com/movie/review?res=9B02E5D8153AF931A25753C1A9649C8B63 www.theguardian.com/film/2002/aug/23/1

www.sfgate.com/movies/article/Holiday-Movies-Acts-of-undying-devotion-2743536.php

Journals and Press Packs

Almodóvar, Pedro. Press Pack www.sonyclassics.com/talktoher/flashwebsite/core/hasFlash.html

BFI Statistical Yearbook 2002. www.bfi.org.uk/sites/bfi.org.uk/files/downloads/uk-film-council-film-in-the-uk-2002-statistical-yearbook.pdf. 14

Butler, Judith. (Dec., 1988) *Performative Acts and Gender Constitution: An Essay in Phenomenology and Feminist Theory* Theatre Journal, Vol. 40, No. 4. 524.

Guse, Annette. (Nov 2007, Vol. 43 Issue 4) *Talk to Her! Look at her! Pina Bausch in Pedro Almodóvar's Hable con Ella*. Journal of Germanic Studies.

Mulvey, Laura. (1975) - *Visual Pleasure and Narrative Cinema*. Screen 16.3 Autumn 1975.

Interesting non-Almodóvar films to compare *Talk to Her* with:

Her (2013 Dir. Spike Jonze)

Lars and the Real Girl (2007 Dir. Craig Gillespie)

One Hour Photo (2002 Dir. Mark Romanek)

Psycho (1960 Dir. Alfred Hitchcock)

Rear Window (1954 Dir. Alfred Hitchcock)

Viridiana (1960 Dir. Luis Buñuel)

What Women Want (2000 Dir. Nancy Myers)

ALSO AVAILABLE

Studying Pan's Labyrinth
Tanya Jones

**Studying
The Devil's Backbone**
James Rose

ALSO AVAILABLE

Studying Fight Club
Mark Ramey

Studying City of God
Stephanie Muir

Printed and bound by CPI Group (UK) Ltd, Croydon, CR0 4YY

13/04/2025

14656601-0005